TOMMO

TOMMO

TO BUSY TO DIE

DEREK THOMPSON

RACING POST

This edition first published in Great Britain in 2013 by Racing Post Books
Raceform, Compton, Newbury, Berkshire, RG20 6NL

1 3 5 7 9 10 8 6 4 2

A catalogue record for this book is available from the British Library.

ISBN 978-1-909471-03-0
Kindle ISBN 978-1-909471-19-1
Epub ISBN 978-1-909471-20-7

Cover designed by Jay Vincent
Book designed by Soapbox
www.soapbox.co.uk

Printed and bound by the CPI Group (UK) Ltd, Croydon, CR0 4YY

Every effort has been made to fulfil requirements with regard to copyright
material. The author and publisher will be glad to rectify any omissions at the
earliest opportunity.

www.racingpost.com/shop

CONTENTS

DEDICATION

I always wanted to dedicate this book to my father, Stanley, but I found it difficult to put my feelings into words. Then mum directed me towards a letter sent to her in 1983 by Tom Stone, who was secretary of the Teesside Apollo Male Voice Choir, of which dad was chairman. The letter, written in November 1983 following dad's death, sums up what I thought about him better than I ever could.

Tom wrote: 'This is probably the most difficult task I have had to perform for many years.

'It is not easy to know just where to begin to offer you not only my own heartfelt thoughts, but also those of all the choir at the passing of your husband and our chairman and our friend, for a friend to all of us is just what Stan was on every possible occasion.

'It will be some time yet before it will really sink in that we must accept it as a hard solid fact that we will not hear his cheerful quips, his kind inquiry for anyone who was not well, his encouragement in all the choir attempted to do and possibly the thing we appreciated most, his constructive ideas which never failed to bear fruit.

'His enthusiasm rubbed off on to everyone with the result that we reached heights hitherto undreamed of and any failures we had were not seen as such but as a challenge for the next time.'

Derek Thompson, August 2013

FOREWORD
by Bob Champion

I have known and been friends with Derek since he was four years old. His ambition has always been to try to be as good a commentator as Sir Peter O'Sullivan, which I think he has almost achieved.

Tommo is so hard working and I am sure he wishes there was sometimes nine days in a week!

When he was told he had cancer it was at the same time he was kept in suspense as to whether he would be involved with the new Channel 4 Racing team, I know he found both these events soul destroying and these were obviously very low points in his life, but being Tommo he has bounced back.

As you read this you will see the two sides of Tommo. He is certainly a real fighter, and his autobiography is an excellent and true read. Enjoy!

Bob Champion MBE

INTRODUCTION
by Jeremy Kyle

As he never tires of telling us, Derek Thompson is Mr. Racing. He is the Voice of Racing too, even if he does say so himself. And he does. Often.

An institution and a legend … is how he likes to refer to himself. And as such, he's someone who should have pockets deeper than the drop at Becher's Brook. But as many of us in the racing community are so often made aware, Tommo just doesn't have the long arms to match those deep pockets.

There is literally no beginning to Tommo's generosity. His parsimony is truly the stuff of legend. I'm never sure if times are tight or if he just is – either way, there's about as much chance of him buying the next round of drinks as there is of me buying a copy of this book!

But what a book. And what a choice of man to help him peddle it. Why me you might ask? The truth is nobody else would do it. And of those who did say 'yes', I'm probably the only one who didn't charge.

But I've taken the job now and I will do what I can to help sell this book. I guess I could tell you of all Tommo's tales. I could speak of the scars and the scandal from his 30 years at the helm of Channel 4 Racing. I could tempt and tease with the best of his 'I was there' stories, and wax long and lyrical about the people and places to which Tommo has had access down the years. But why should I, when he's about to bang on for the next 280-odd pages doing just that himself?

No, Derek Thompson basically wants me to help him sell his book. And I shall. Here's why I think you should buy it. There's no doubting the man's place in racing folklore. There's no doubting the fact that he's lived an interesting life, having been there and done it through some of the highest highs and the lowest lows of the sport I love – often contributing to both. Say what you like about Tommo (the chances are he's said exactly what he likes – and doesn't – about you in this book) but the man's a battler and a stayer too. As someone who has faced his demons through cancer, just like Tommo, I say that with genuine conviction and sincerity.

It is with that same conviction and sincerity that I implore you to buy this book. Please, have your friends buy the book too. In fact have them buy ten. Because the more copies of this damned thing we shift, the less likely it is that his friends will keep getting stiffed for his tab at dinner.

Go to it – do your duty!

Jeremy Kyle, London, 2013

PROLOGUE

There was a brief pause while he perused the notes. Nobody said a word. There was not a thing I could think of to say, which was unusual for me. For well over 40 years I have been paid to use my mouth. Put a microphone in my hand and I can talk, even when there's nothing obvious to talk about. But this time, perhaps for the first time, I did not want to talk. I wanted to listen. So I waited and I listened.

Eventually, after what felt like an eternity, he raised his head from the notes and looked at us. Then he spoke.

'You've got cancer.'

That was all he said, at least I think it was. If he said anything more I didn't hear it. Three words drowned out everything else.

People wonder what it must be like to be given that sort of news. You see people being told they have cancer on television programmes and in films. You even hear of friends and work colleagues who have been in the very same position, but it doesn't happen to you, except that, of course, it does. It happens to lots of us and now it what was happening to me. I was in the surgery of Mr Richard Miller, a colorectal surgeon based at Addenbrooke's Hospital. This, it turned out, was my turn.

'We want you in for the operation straightaway,' he said. Julie squeezed my hand, the tiniest gesture from wife to husband, but one that meant so much. In moments like this it helps to know there is someone there for you.

'The good news is that we've had a cancellation for tomorrow so I'd like you to get yourself ready to have the operation in the morning.'

That second piece of news disturbed me almost as much as the first.

'I'm sorry Doc,' I said. I knew he was a surgeon, not a doctor, but I called him Doc all the same. Anything less seemed disrespectful.

'I'm afraid I can't possibly come in tomorrow,' I explained, an earnest expression on my face. 'It's Royal Ascot this week. I've had to give up half a day's work just to come here. Is there any chance I can have the op next week instead?'

Julie looked at me in the way she had looked at me more than once in the past. It wasn't a good look. Even Mr Miller seemed a bit taken aback.

'Okay,' he said. 'We can leave it a week but we absolutely cannot leave it for two. You're in next week.'

I knew that meant the following week would be a write-off but at least I could work for the remainder of Royal Ascot. That's where I had been that morning. At 7am, as usual, I had arrived at the track. Ascot was a BBC course, so there were no Channel 4 duties there for me to fulfil, but At The Races covered the royal meeting and At The Races was one of my many teams. So I had driven from Newmarket to Ascot, leaving at not long after 5am and getting there just as the racecourse was waking up to the first of the five most important days in Flat racing. Frankel would be there that afternoon. I would not, but at least I was there for the morning.

At 7.05am a few of the card's runners walked from the race-course stables to the track for their morning exercise and a pick of grass. You could usually rely on most of the international contingent coming out for a stretching of legs around then, so I was there as well, ready and waiting to interview any trainers or stable lads that were up for a chat with Tommo. I spoke to one 'big fella' after another, interviews in the can, ready to be played out from 9am when At The Races began its Ascot build-up. By the time Catt and Big Mac started the opening programme of the day I must have done seven or eight interviews, more than enough to merit a quick break for a bacon sandwich.

As the morning went on there were more interviews, some broadcast live, some recorded for future consumption. From 11.30am onwards the jockeys and trainers began to arrive, not to mention some of the celebrities for whom Ascot and a free lunch are powerful magnets. I spoke to one after the other, cracking a few jokes, having a few laughs, doing what I do. Then, with my television requirements for the day completed, I did something else that I do quite a lot of and went to a private box to give a talk. This time it was for William Hill, the owners of more than 2,500 betting shops, most of which I've probably opened. This time I was talking to a different sort of punter, but I was still talking, so I was as comfortable as ever.

I always like coming into this particular box because I'm friendly with the chef who cooks the lunches. He also cooks for Simon Cowell in the box next door. I guarantee that if you ever get invited to lunch by Simon Cowell you are certain to eat well. The chef also works for the McLaren Formula One team. I asked him once what the drivers have for breakfast. Do you know what he told me? A full English. That surprised me and I'm sure it surprised you as well. It's the sort of little nugget that I use in after-dinner speeches. I do quite a few of those, too.

On this occasion it wasn't a speech, just a little chat in a corporate box. Dead easy. I had a stooge as well, Frankel's jockey Tom Queally, who was also on William Hill's books. I know full well that Tom does not particularly like me, and I wouldn't be his biggest fan, either, but we were both being paid so putting on an act wasn't hard. I wished Tom the very best of luck on Frankel – not that he would ever have needed it on a horse like Frankel – and instigated a round of applause for our special guest.

Goodbyes completed, I was off. I walked into the car park and headed for the Mercedes. People said hello and I said hello back, confirming to their astonishment that I was indeed leaving just as they were arriving.

'Things to do,' I told them, which was true. It wasn't even the first time I'd left Royal Ascot before racing started. A couple of years earlier I had worked there for At The Races in the morning before driving 180 miles to Carmarthenshire's Ffos Las racecourse to host Tommo TV at its very first meeting. I didn't leave there until after 9pm but I was still back at Ascot, ready to record, at 7am the following morning.

But this time I wasn't going to a racecourse in Wales but to a hospital in Cambridge. The colonoscopy had been done a week earlier at the instigation of my own doctor, Simon Arthur. The appointment with Mr Miller was arranged almost immediately afterwards. Julie had been a nurse. She knew that I had to get myself checked out. For a while I had been seeing bits of red in my poo. I'm not a big lover of beetroot so it had to be blood. I thought I had known what the problem might be. Many years ago when I was riding as an amateur jump jockey I suffered a bit from haemorrhoids. It's not a nice thing to admit to in print, but there you have it. In those days the piles were a real problem to me, but I just put it down to wet saddles and riding out in jeans. The problem went away, although years later I moved with my second wife to the Buckinghamshire town of Chalfont St Giles. I have to admit that used to make me chuckle.

These days Newmarket is my home and I collected Julie from there on the way to Addenbrooke's. As we drove towards the hospital I switched on BBC Radio 5 live. I once spent a significant chunk of my life working for BBC Radio and I would be returning to the fold less than a year later. I listened to Frankel routing the Queen Anne Stakes field, but by the time the runners for the following King's Stand Stakes were being loaded into the stalls I was sat with Julie waiting to be called into Mr Miller's office.

A few minutes later I was told I had cancer. Fortunately I'm too busy to die. I told myself that as I left the hospital. Then I started thinking about the Wednesday card at Ascot. The operation was still a week away. I parked all thoughts of it somewhere in the back of my mind and concentrated on work. That was easier than you might think because work comes first. Always had done. Pleased to report, it still does.

ONE

'I WANT TO BE PETER O'SULLEVAN!'

When I was born, Tommo was not. He came later, the name at least. Back then I was just Derek. To a very small group of people I still am.

I've lived so long as Tommo that it's hard to know where Derek stops and Tommo starts. If you asked me if I put on an act, if I pretend to be something I'm not, if the person you see on television is a self-created persona, I would say no. I would say that I am what I am, and what I am is what you see. Not everyone would agree, though. Some of those closest to me – but not all of them – reckon that the man they know and love is a very different person to the man you watch with a microphone in his hand walking around a racecourse, opening a betting shop or queuing in the supermarket. I have my view and they have theirs. I would like to think I'm right but when you're trying to define yourself as a person is your opinion any more valid than those who know you best? Maybe the real me is Derek. Maybe the real me is Tommo. What I can tell you with absolute certainty is that when I entered the world in Stockton-on-Tees on 31 July 1950, I was definitely Derek. I stayed that way for many years.

I've been fortunate enough to interview many wonderful people over the years but I can't imagine many were more impressive than my parents. It has become fashionable to lament your upbringing and to highlight all the things that were wrong in the way you were brought up. I can't do that. I was blessed. Mum and dad, Stanley and Lillian Thompson, could not have done more for me. They were perfect parents, generous, caring and supportive. By the time I came along they had already had some practice as my brother Howard was born three years before me. And do you know what? Howard was also the perfect brother and in Bob Champion I had the perfect best mate. I was one lucky lad.

Stanley Moorhouse Thompson played a major role in shaping me into the person I became. When I think of dad I see a lot of him in me. For a start he adored racing and trained a few horses, some of which gave me my first rides as a jockey. He was also a great family man, which I'd like to think I am, and he was fascinated by broadcasting. There is, however, one crucial way in which we differ. My father was a hero, a man who fought for his country in the most courageous way imaginable. He risked his life on numerous occasions. Compared to what he did in the most dangerous years of his life, I live a very frivolous existence.

When dad was a lad he certainly did not. His father was a drunk but his father was all he had. Dad's mother died when he was a young boy. He grew up with no mother and also no sister because she was given away for adoption. My grandfather couldn't afford to bring her up. When you're paying for a lot of beer it's hard to support one child, let alone two. My parents gave Howard and I everything we could possibly have wanted. Dad, on the other hand, got very little of what he wanted or even needed from his only surviving parent. Back then they lived in South London. Truth be told, Grandad Thompson lived in the pub. He spent a lot of hours inside the pub while his son spent a lot of hours stood outside the pub waiting to help his father home. As he got older he started selling copies of the London *Evening Standard* on the road. He was one of the 'read all about it' men. A little while later he was one of the bravest men.

Dad became a flight sergeant in RAF Bomber Command during the Second World War. As part of the Pathfinders Squadron he was one of the team responsible for dropping the flares over Germany that helped the Wellington bombers find their targets. It must have been a terrifying time, but although some of what he went through left terrible mental scars, he was happy to tell the stories of what he had experienced during his 40 sorties. He once told us how the plane he was in crashed. He had to be dragged out but amazingly he was in one piece and hardly hurt at all. Luck was on his side that day.

Luck was also on his side the day he met the lady who became his wife. Stanley Moorhouse Thompson and Lillian May Forster were married during the war in 1943. Mum was born and brought up as a north east girl through and through, and to this day she still lives in the same town, Nunthorpe, just outside Middlesbrough, where she raised her boys. She was an old-fash-ioned type of mother in that she believed her place was in the home, both to support her husband and to look after her children. She was outstanding at both jobs but mum did not only believe that she had a duty to her family. She also felt she had a duty to her community. She was a local councillor and chair-woman of the education committee. That's not all, though, because she became deputy mayor of Teesside and, as an added bonus, enjoyed the privilege of being in the party that escorted the Queen during her visit to the area in the Silver Jubilee year of 1977. But the Queen was far from the only person of note that mum knew. She was once a regular babysitter of another local lad, Ridley Scott, who went on to be an Oscar-winning film director. Sadly, when he made his acceptance speech after being named best director for the movie *Gladiator*, he forget to mention mum, but it was an emotional time for Ridley so we can forgive him.

If you ask my mum now what she remembers most about me as a little boy, it's that I was apparently a climber. Evidently I would climb anything. She thought I was going to be a mountaineer. When I was aged two she once realised to her horror that I had disappeared. A frantic search didn't last long. I was found on the roof of the car. I'd be lying if I said I have a first-hand recollection of that. There is, however, still something in my head that takes me back to a very unpleasant incident that occurred when I was four and a half years old.

When I look back to my childhood years almost all the memories are good. This is one of the very few bad ones. Howard and I had gone out to play. One of our favourite games was cowboys and Indians, which we used to play in a field behind the house. It engrossed us for hours. Whether you're a cowboy or an Indian you need a good fire but the one we had built that fateful day was a bit pathetic. We decided to stamp it out and start another. Once I started stamping it became clear that another was not going to be built. I was wearing a pair of little wellington boots that mum still has to this day. She has them as a reminder of what happened the last time I wore them.

For almost 60 years they have had a singe up the side. That's because as soon as I attempted to put out the burning embers the wellies seemed to act like a flare. Thereafter I learnt the cruel but valuable lesson that you must never try to put out a bonfire while wearing long cotton trousers. Very unfortunately, I had been having trouble with the trousers. They were always falling down so before dad had gone to work I asked him to tie a double knot in them. How I wish I had not asked him to do that. My trousers caught fire and so did the legs inside them. Howard managed to pull me away but by the time he did so I had burnt myself pretty badly. Howard somehow was able to pull off the trousers but it took longer than it should have done because of the blasted double knot. Wearing nothing more than my underpants from the waste down, I ran home. It was the last time I would do that for a long time.

Fortunately my face was unharmed but just behind the knee I was quite seriously damaged. As a result of my stupidity I spent exactly 100 days in hospital. To make matters worse, I contracted measles in hospital and had to be put in solitary confinement. All mum and dad could do when they came to visit was look at me through a glass window. I still feel as though I missed out on the cuddles. It was such a traumatic time. I even upset the matron, which in a 1950s hospital was never a good idea. This large buxom lady would come round every day at the same time, stand at the end of the bed and say: 'Good morning, and how are you?' She used the same words every time. One morning, thinking she would see it as a joke, I got in there first and when she arrived by my bed, I said: 'Good morning, and how are you?'

She didn't laugh.

'Right,' she said. 'No more sweets for you for a week.' She was true to her word. Little Derek got not a single sweetie for a whole week. I've never forgotten that, nor what it was like to be in hospital for so long, but the length of my incarceration was understandable. The repair job was immense. The surgeons had to take skin from the top of my leg and put it on the back of my scorched knee. To this day I still have a scar as a reminder of what happened. For years my poor leg needed constant lubrication. Mum tells me that she spent much of my childhood having to deal with greasy pyjamas. I'm pleased to say that my wife Julie does not have the same problem.

Burning your leg and spending more than three months in hospital represents a major blow to a young boy. It put a halt on me continuing my love of the outdoors but soon enough I was back in the open air, greatly encouraged by dad. It was because of mum that dad ended up in the north east of England. Mum was initially from Jarrow – in fact she had family members who took part in the famous Jarrow March of 1936 – and when she and dad got together they wanted to spend their life together in what is a very special part of the country. Dad became a north east man through and through and, like mum, a real member of his local community. In his youth he had been an enthusiastic long-distance walker but as he got older he began to move faster. He became a keen and talented runner. Thanks to dad, both Howard and I developed an interest in athletics, but we were never as talented as dad, although I wasn't bad at the high jump. At his peak dad could run a mile in four minutes and 20 seconds, and that was before Roger Bannister made history when the world record for the distance was four minutes and five seconds. He became chairman of the Middlesbrough and Cleveland Harriers and later president of the northern branch of the Amateur Athletic Association. Dad loved his running but he also fancied talking about running as well, so much so that in the early 1950s he applied for a broadcasting job with the BBC in Manchester. He didn't get it but the man who did turned out to be pretty useful. His name was David Coleman.

But it wasn't only watching athletes run that dad enjoyed. He also loved watching horses run. And it was because of dad that I developed a passion for horses. It was a passion that would shape the rest of my life.

According to mum I first sat on a pony at the age of two. By that stage Howard, three years my elder, was already quite proficient thanks to considerable encouragement from dad. Where Stanley Thompson's love of horses came from I don't really know, but it was definitely there and thanks to his success at business he was able to purchase ponies for us to ride. The money used to pay for the ponies came from steel. At the end of the war he decided that steel was the way forward. A bit like a young Alan Sugar, he would go to Middlesbrough railway station and make calls from the phone box to people he thought might need steel. If they said they did he would ring someone else and ask if they had any steel to sell. If they had the steel he would buy it and then sell it on at a profit. At that stage he was no more than a middle man but it was a system that worked. By 1950 he was able to start his own business as a steel stockist and on the day after I was born 'S M Thompson Ltd' came into existence. It survives to this day with Howard in charge of what is now a steel stockholding and processing company. If you're based in the north east and require a bit of flame cutting, plasma cutting, laser cutting, bevel cutting, plate marking, plate rolling, section rolling, press braking or drilling, or if you just need some steel, then S M Thompson Ltd is the place to go. I can heartily recommend it. It's very good steel indeed.

Luckily for Howard and I, some of the money that dad made from steel enabled us to have ponies. They weren't particularly expensive ponies but you could get quite a bit in those days for £25, and £25 was more than enough to buy us animals that brought us enormous pleasure. They also provided the link between the two Thompson brothers and the man who would become a lifelong best friend to both Howard and myself.

We met Bob Champion through the Cleveland Hounds, the pack we hunted with from a young age. Bob's father was the huntsman and Bob was an exceptionally competent young rider. We quickly became great friends. The three of us and another mate called Timmy Hill joined the local pony club and often attended horse shows. We would ride our ponies on the roads, we rode them up a north east landmark called Rosebery Topping and we even rode them to school, which you were allowed to do in those days. These days kids take mobile phones to school. We took ponies. For me the school was Guisborough Grammar School, where I went after spending a few years before that at a boarding school in the North York Moors National Park called Fyling Hall. As I got older I became pretty competent as a show jumper. I won the Durham County Junior Championships on the same day Harvey Smith won the seniors' event. I was tenth in the national championships and also once third in a pony class at the hallowed show jumping ground that is Hickstead. Sadly, I never got to ride down its famous Derby Bank. I would have enjoyed that.

Not that our time together was only about ponies. During the long school summer holidays we were always in and out of each other's houses. Bob's family lived about five miles from us and we were forever spending time on the number 58 bus going to and from our respective homes. The three of us were always doing something together. We often went to watch wrestling at a big hall in Middlesbrough's Cannon Street, part of an area that was subsequently bulldozed. We played on motorbikes in fields and we also enjoyed seeing as many films as we could at the cinema. I remember we once went to see the 1959 adventure movie *North West Frontier*, starring Lauren Bacall and Kenneth More. We loved it. In fact we loved it so much that we decided that if we stayed in our seats at the end of the film we could watch it all over again at the next showing. And we did. Unfortunately, what we hadn't reckoned on was that by extending our trip to the cinema we missed the last bus home. Dad had to come and collect us. He wasn't pleased.

He was, however, happy to encourage our interest in racing. I reckon I was probably aged eight when dad took me to our local racecourse, Stockton, for the first time. What a day that was. Immediately I was hooked on the sport. I have to admit that this instant infatuation was helped by the fact dad let me have a four-shilling bet on every race. I took the bookies to the cleaners! At the end of the afternoon my bets had won me £9, 16 shillings and sixpence. And then to put the seal on a wonderful day we had a fish and chips supper on the way home. I still love fish and chips to this day.

After that I couldn't get enough of racing. I was totally hooked. Everything I could find out about the sport was devoured. Anything that was written about racing was read and whenever there was racing on television that I could watch, I watched it. I became a walking form book. Back in those days there tended to be only two meetings a day, so it was much easier to keep abreast of everything that was going on. Most of all I loved going racing, which I did as often as I could. When there was a Stockton meeting on a non school day I would get the bus that went to the track and when nobody was watching I would climb over the wall and get into the racecourse, which I shouldn't have been able to do without an adult.

Very often I wasn't alone. Howard liked to come along and so did Bob. And we didn't only go to Stockton. Redcar was another of our favourite racecourses. It was there, at the track that has a graveyard as its next door neighbour, that I made my television debut. Bob's dad also used to drive the knacker man's wagon and so we sometimes got a lift to the track. That's how we got there one afternoon when racing from Redcar was being broadcast on ITV. When we went to Redcar we almost always stood near the ITV broadcast position, which overlooked the paddock. On this particular occasion John Rickman was presenting the coverage and we ended up talking to him live on air. I think somebody must have failed to turn up for a pre-arranged interview, or perhaps he was just intrigued by the three lads standing a few yards away. When he called us over we didn't need to be asked twice. John asked all of us what we wanted to be when we grew up. Howard said he wanted to take over his father's firm. Bob said he wanted to be a jockey. And me? I said I wanted to be the next Peter O'Sullevan. Any extra details have disappeared from my memory but Bob insists I also told John that I wanted to work for the BBC because the BBC was better than ITV!

I find it very hard to believe that I could have been so insensitive but that's how Bob remembers a conversation that was recorded on a tape long since wiped clean. It might not exist anymore but the three boys turned out to have pretty good eyes to the future. Howard did indeed take over dad's business. Bob did indeed become a jockey and I did indeed work for the BBC, and also for ITV and then Channel 4. My ambition to become a broadcaster was fulfilled. So, too, was my ambition to become a jockey. It has to be said, however, that I was considerably better at one than the other.

TWO

REPEATEDLY FALLING OFF HORSES

t is a trend these days for many of our top sport broadcasters to have been former practitioners of the sport they broadcast about. At the BBC Gary Lineker, an ex-footballer, is the main football presenter, Steve Cram, an ex-athlete, is the main athletics commentator and Andrew Castle, an ex-tennis player, is the main tennis commentator. It isn't a compulsory requirement – you might not be surprised to learn that John McCririck was never a jockey – but I was, in some ways, a trendsetter. I dabbled at two of racing's main professions before deciding to stop dabbling and start working at something I could actually do. I was a failed trainer (assistant) and a failed jockey (amateur) before I became a broadcaster (available).

As with so much in my life I have dad to thank for giving me the push that allowed me to experience being both a jockey and trainer. Having said that, some of the experiences dad gave me as a jockey I could probably have done without. Had I been half a century later I would have spent many of my early teen years taking part on the pony racing circuit that is now so popular with so many children in Britain having been a big thing in Ireland for years. When I was growing up that opportunity did not exist. I went through the pony club ranks, hunted and took part in show-jumping classes but I wanted to have a crack at riding racehorses in races. What I lacked was racehorses. Dad helped out with that.

Howard was just as keen as me to try his luck as a jockey, so dad had taken out a permit to train horses that would run in his ownership. Howard had been having great fun riding in a few point-to-point races with me often acting as stable lad, leading Howard and his mount around the paddock in the countdown to the off. I loved that. It meant I was finally involved in racing. Apart from Howard, dad and Bob, nobody in racing really knew I existed, but I was now, even in a very small way, involved in the racing game. I felt part of the sport, but I wanted my part in the sport to increase. On a memorable afternoon at the Sedgefield point-to-point it did.

The horse's name was Louise Profit. Dad trained her – although I was doing a lot of the training work myself – and she gave me my first ever ride in a race. I'll never forget it. What an experience. It was absolutely horrible.

Even cantering down to the start it didn't feel right. The horse didn't feel right. I didn't feel right. I felt nervous. Scared even. Up to that point I had very rarely been frightened. Not really. But now I was. Circling around at the start along with the other jockeys felt surreal. Was this really me? And if it was, why the hell was it? What was I letting myself in for? I couldn't understand it. I had never been nervous riding at full speed up the gallops, nor when jumping all manner of fences out hunting. I had ridden against the clock in showjumping when the merest nudge of a rail could make the difference between winning and losing. That hadn't troubled me. This did. I tried to make sense of it in my head. Perhaps it was the cold weather. Then I realised that where we lived it was nearly always cold. I convinced myself – or tried to – that once the starter let us go it would all be different. To a degree it was different. It was worse.

Louise Profit set off like a mare who had just felt a red-hot poker on her backside. 'Whoa girl! Whoa! Whoa!' Nothing I said made any difference. Sadly, I was making things worse. Due to my nerves I seemed to have lost all the strength in my arms. I'm sure that if I had been relaxed, as I always had been on a horse, she would have responded to my request and settled. Instead she went off towards the first fence at what felt like 50 miles per hour. I had never been so fast on a horse in my entire life. Even before that first fence was jumped I knew there and then that I no longer wanted to be a jockey. Unfortunately by then it was too late.

You will not be surprised to learn we did not win. You might be surprised to learn we did finish. Louise Profit might have appeared a bit wild but she also had a sense of self-preservation. She ended the race on her feet and with me out on mine. I was utterly exhausted. As I dismounted and my toes touched the ground my legs went to jelly. How I managed to stay upright I'll never know. Had I been seen by Bob, who by now was doing very well indeed on the amateur circuit, I would have been deeply embarrassed.

Fortunately, I've always been very good at overcoming embarrassment. Strangely, I also seemed to overcome my nerves, or at least to put them to one side. I had survived, and on the basis that I would have looked a proper big girl's blouse if I'd retired in terror after a single ride, I carried on. So I continued riding and started falling.

I fell a little more regularly than I would have liked to have done from a horse named Grand Corton. Dad arrived home with him one day following a trip to the bloodstock sales at Ascot, where some of racing's bargain basement offerings could be snapped up at a reasonable price. Grand Corton, however, did not come cheap. To bring him north dad had paid £500, which was no small sum in the late 1960s. I asked dad what his form was like? He had no idea.

'I didn't need to look at his form,' he said. 'Look at the horse. He's lovely Derek.'

I agreed that he was lovely but to my horror he wasn't just lovely. He was clumsy. As soon as I picked up a copy of the form book I could see straightaway that dad had bought a horse who had something of a death wish. Worse still, the kamikaze gelding had been bought for me to ride.

'Dad, there's a picture of him on the front cover,' I said.

Dad thought this was a good thing. But it was not. It was a bad thing. The picture was of Grand Corton sending his jockey into orbit in what appeared to be one of the most spectacular falls I had ever seen. A quick inspection of Grand Corton's form made clear that this had not been the first fall of his life. It wouldn't be his last, either.

It was clearly a bad sign when on our first start together at Catterick we were involved in an accident before the race had even started. Dad had entered us in a two-mile amateur riders' chase, the start for which was in a chute at the top of the home straight. Perhaps because I was already trying to work out in which hospital I would be spending the rest of the day, I found it impossible to apply the brakes as we closed in on the corrugated iron fence at the back of the two-mile start. The horse, who very probably had trouble with his eyesight, seemed completely unaware of the buffers that he was cantering towards and crashed straight into them. This did at least bring him to a halt.

By the age of 17 I'd learnt plenty of swear words and Grand Corton was giving me good reason to use them. After brushing myself down, apologising profusely for causing a delay and then getting remounted, I realised there was a sense of inevitability about what was going to happen. I wasn't wrong. The tapes went up and Grand Corton went off. Like a rocket. It was Louise Profit at Sedgefield all over again. Grand Corton, for all his faults, did not lack enthusiasm. What he did lack was the ability to get over a fence. Thundering at speed on the downhill run to Catterick's first fence I would have put my hands together and prayed had that been possible without letting go of the reins. Just as he had failed to notice the corrugated iron fence, Grand Corton seemed totally oblivious to the big black fence that he smashed into at full pelt. The obstacle appeared to wave a white flag of surrender and let Grand Corton through, but by this point I was soaring through the North Yorkshire air on a one-way trip to some North Yorkshire grass. Not long after landing on the grass I became a human football for the horses behind me, who kicked me one after the other. Thanks to Grand Corton I had been knocked unconscious.

Fortunately, I wasn't out cold for long. When I came round astonishingly I was in one piece. Not so lucky were the riding boots I had borrowed from one of the weighing-room valets, whose job it is to look after the jockeys. The boots had been torn to shreds, although I'm not sure how. Working out how on earth

I was going to pay for a new pair quickly brought me back to my senses.

Part of my brain must have been at least temporarily affected because that was not the last time I rode Grand Corton. Dad felt that maybe it was just fences that were the problem. To test the theory he entered him for another race at Catterick, but this time over hurdles. To say I had my reservations would be an understatement but I duly went to Catterick and once again got on the back of the horse who had left me seeing stars a few weeks earlier. This time we survived the trip to the start. We even survived the first flight of hurdles. I'd like to say that we survived the second but I'd be lying.

Just as in his previous race Grand Corton set off like the clappers, but the fact that he had negotiated the first hurdle made me think that dad might have been right. The poor lad's stumbling block could have been that he disliked fences and had been hankering after hurdles. It was a fair theory but it came unstuck in dramatic fashion at the second flight. It would be unfair on Grand Corton to say that he did anything wrong in his jumping of the hurdle because he never actually jumped it. Instead, while a good 20 lengths clear of the field, he came to within a stride of the obstacle and veered right, crashing out through the plastic rails that guide the horses into the hurdle. As before, he did not take me with him, but this time I managed to remain conscious. That was the good bit. The bad bit was that I had landed on my bum on the take-off side of the hurdle. Somehow the horse had ejected me from the saddle and, like an Olympic gymnast, I had twisted through the air and on to the ground. My back was leaning against the hurdle and my front was facing what to my eyes looked like a Catterick reincarnation of the charge of the light brigade. Somehow I survived again.

For some reason I still hadn't learned my lesson. The moment of complete realisation came at Sedgefield on a Boxing Day when I partnered a horse for trainer Taffy Williams. Its form figures read like a string of duck eggs, one zero after another, indicating that it had finished miles behind the winner in all its races. The horse was not the next Arkle, that much was clear, yet Taffy was strangely confident.

'This will win,' he said as he legged me up in the paddock. I thought he was pulling my leg. But he wasn't.

'This horse will win,' he repeated. 'All right? We've backed him. Don't mess it up.'

You might think why on earth would a trainer who had readied a horse for months to pull off a gamble employ an amateur jockey with no wins but plenty of falls to his name. One reason was that on a Boxing Day back then there were sometimes ten or more meetings. That meant finding a decent rider could be difficult. Even finding a bad one could be tricky. Another reason is that bookmakers who saw Mr D Thompson riding an apparently useless chaser would not think twice about offering meaty odds. And meaty odds were exactly what Taffy wanted.

By now you've probably guessed that we fell, and we did, but it genuinely was not my fault. On the way down to the start I encountered a new feeling. I was sat on the back of a horse in the minutes leading up to a race and I was hopeful. Taffy was right. Sometimes you only need to be going at a slow pace to get a feel for a horse's ability and this horse felt good. There was a touch of

19

class about him, and in a moderate race at Sedgefield on Boxing Day, a touch of class would be more than enough.

My final instructions had been to sit handy in second or third, take the lead turning for home, kick on and win. As the race started I kept Taffy's instructions at the front of my mind and settled the horse close to the inside running rail in third. Within seconds I knew my fate, but not for long as I was knocked unconscious. As we jumped the fence, the horse on our immediate outside cannoned into us and practically landed on my lad. We were beaten up in mid-air and both of us were crunched to ground that was cold, frosty and hard. Race over. Gamble not landed. Oh heck.

By the time I regained consciousness the runners were not long off jumping the fence on their second circuit. I saw them jumping it from the stretcher that the ambulance team had put me on. Back in the racecourse medical room, although a little dazed, I could clearly hear the voice of Taffy Williams. He didn't sound in a very good mood and he didn't seem especially keen to pass on his best wishes. In those days, races like that one at Sedgefield received no sort of television coverage. All Taffy knew was what he had seen in the distance through binoculars. The facts in his head were that his heavily backed horse had fallen at the first fence and I had been the man riding him when it happened.

'Bloody useless amateur,' he said. 'You'll never ride for me again.'

Fair play to Taffy, he was true to his word. I didn't ride for him again but I didn't ride for many people again. In total I had around 70 rides as an amateur. I never won a race and never really came close. Until many years down the line, on a right royal day at Plumpton, fourth in a little contest at Newcastle was the best I could manage. Tommy Stack rode the winner of that Newcastle race and he went on to rather better things aboard a chaser called Red Rum.

Long before he was famous I met Red Rum myself. I was at Wetherby to lead up Howard, who very bravely was there to ride Louise Profit for dad. I was getting the horse tacked up in the racecourse stables when my eye was drawn to a gorgeous girl in the next-door box.

'Hello,' I said. 'How are you?' She said she was fine, which encouraged me to ask another question.

'What's the name of your horse? Any good?'

'No, not really,' she said. 'He's called Red Rum.'

We all know what happened to Red Rum, but even now, all those years later, I still wonder what happened to that gorgeous girl.

Having a brief spell as an amateur jump jockey, however unspectacular, has left me forever in awe of those who risk their lives on a daily basis riding over fences and hurdles. Whether they are great champions like Tony McCoy and John Francome, or riders who ply their trade on the bottom rung of the ladder, they are brave men and women, one and all. In fact, among sportsmen they are the bravest. In no other sport do you get followed by an ambulance. Anyone who ever places a bet on a horse or goes to the races should be grateful to jockeys. They will always have my respect because I know from first-hand experience that the job they do is anything but easy. I know the same is true of those who train horses. I know that because training was something else I had a go at and gave up.

At no point was I ever a licensed trained but I did work as an assistant to two excellent trainers, one of them in the north of England, the other in the heart of France's racing community. For me France came second. England came first. That I got to work for both of the trainers was due to dad.

After I left Guisborough Grammar School I knew I wanted to work in racing. I was completely hooked on the sport and taking the odd ride as an amateur only increased my enthusiasm for a life in racing. One avenue that attracted me was broadcasting – more on that soon – but another possibility was trying to become a trainer. I already had experience of the job, albeit at a very minor level, from helping dad with the few horses he kept himself, but that in itself was not going to take me very far. Dad wanted to help and he did. He wrote to as many of the local trainers as he could think of, some of whom he had got to know a bit from being at the races. He offered them my services free of charge. In those days that was perfectly normal. Unless you were born with a silver spoon in your mouth, getting involved in the business of training racehorses was not easy. You had to do a lot of work for little or no financial reward. What you were getting for your labour was not money but vital and precious experience. Denys Smith agreed to give me that experience.

I joined Denys as soon as I'd left school in the early summer of 1968. I was a few weeks off turning 18 and Denys was a few months into being jumping's champion trainer. He had just enjoyed the best season of his career, capped off wonderfully with the triumph of Red Alligator in the Grand National, a victory that came only days before the funeral of his father-in-law. It must have been an emotional time for Denys but there were plenty of them over the years as the best horse he probably ever had, The Grey Bomber, was killed after putting a single foot into a pool of water that electric wires had blown into during a gale. That was a desperate day for Denys but he had plenty more good ones during a career that ran from 1958 to 2002.

Denys, a former cattle dealer, was based not a million miles from the Thompson family home in Bishop Auckland, a market town situated 12 miles from both Durham and Darlington. This was real racing land because only a stone's throw from Denys's Holdforth Farm yard were the stables of the legendary trainer Arthur Stephenson. Both men sent out scores of winners each season and there was a tremendous rivalry between them. My loyalties were with Denys and he was an outstanding man to call boss. He must have had about 100 horses in his care, some of them top-class over jumps but quite a few of them top-class on the Flat as well. Officially I was his assistant trainer – he still calls me that to this day – but in reality I was nothing more than an unpaid stable lad. There haven't been too many instances in my life when I've been happy to do something for nothing but this was one of them – and there were a lot of somethings that had to be done! My routine involved me leaving home at no later than 6am and driving straight to Denys's place, where I would muck out three horses and then ride them up the gallops. Sometimes Denys, who had a fantastic head lad in Tommy Nevin, would need me in the afternoons, and if so that usually involved me going to the races in the horsebox or with one of the jockeys. And what an honour that was.

The jockeys I got to travel with were two of the finest I've ever seen ride a horse. One was Brian Fletcher. Brian had already won one Grand National aboard Red Alligator but he would win two more, in 1973 and 1974, on Red Rum before finishing second on the same horse the following year, after which he lost the ride to Tommy Stack following a disagreement with Ginger McCain. The other jockey I spent plenty of time with as Denys's assistant was Paddy Broderick, who went on to be the regular rider of the mighty Night Nurse, the winner of consecutive Champion Hurdles in 1976 and 1977. If the three of us went to the races together, Brian and Paddy would share the driving with me sat in the back listening to some great stories. Brian and Paddy also had a deal. Whichever one of them rode a winner would buy dinner for the rest of us. I got free dinners for most of my time with Denys. It was wonderful.

On those days when I wasn't needed at the races I would drive back home and earn a few quid by helping dad, who used to send me off here, there and everywhere delivering steel. I'd like to think I was a pretty decent lorry driver and I very much enjoyed it. Most of the time it was a fun job, although there was the odd unfortunate incident, like the time I delivered three tonnes of steel to the wrong place. I can't understand why, but they let me unload it all before telling me that they hadn't ordered it. The steel was meant for the factory on the other side of the road. During the years I've sometimes had to do the odd miserable job and reloading three tonnes of steel on to the back of a lorry was definitely one of them.

That was an exception to the rule, though. Normally working for dad was fantastic. I was the son of the boss but I was also one of the lads and we often spent more time than we should have done playing cards and drinking tea. When I was behind the wheel of a truck I also got to know plenty about Britain's roads, which stood me in good stead for the future. I also became familiar with so many of Britain's best roadside cafes and truckers' stops. I still go into them to this day whenever I fancy a quick bite to eat. Some of the best meals I've ever had have been in transport cafes. I can say from considerable personal experience that they offer quality roadside nourishment at a very reasonable price. And I like that.

I also more than liked Chantilly, even if it took me a little while to understand anything anybody said. Chantilly, just under 25 miles to the north east of central Paris, is home to the French Derby, the French Oaks and many of the best French trainers. It also became home to me for six months when, after nine months with Denys, I moved on to join a trainer called Pierre Sanoner. Like any young assistant I picked up a healthy share of bollock-ings along the way, but leaving Denys's employment (unpaid) was not due to any deterioration of our relationship. It was simply because then, and also now, it was usual for someone learning to be a trainer to get experience with as many people as possible, ideally in various environments. Dad was well aware of this, so after I completed my service with Denys he began writing to a few trainers in France, one of whom, Pierre, kindly replied and offered me a job.

Chantilly and Bishop Auckland were not exactly similar. In the late 1960s you would have struggled to find a croissant in Bishop Auckland but, at the same time, it wasn't easy to get your teeth around a proper meat pie in Chantilly. Pierre was a lovely old-fash-ioned gentleman. He certainly wasn't one of France's leading trainers but he was respected and rightly so. One of Pierre's claims to fame was that he briefly trained the triple Champion Hurdle winner Persian War when his slightly controversial owner Henry Alper decided that some French air would prove beneficial. I'm not sure it did a great deal to influence Persian War's fortunes but it did me no harm and I really enjoyed my time in Chantilly. We started work at five o'clock every morning and had all the horses mucked out within an hour. The first lot of horses went out to exercise at 6am and on a normal day we would each ride four horses every morning. It was hard work but there were many positives, none more enjoyable than getting the chance to ride around Chantilly's famous racecourse, set against the backdrop of a glorious chateau, alongside Pierre's then stable jockey Wally Swinburn, the father of the man who became synonymous with Shergar, 'the choirboy', Walter Swinburn.

Sad to report, my Chantilly accommodation was about as far removed from the magnificent chateau as it would have been possible to get. I lived in a small room above the stables. Some homes probably have bigger broom cupboards than my French digs. The toilet was a hole in the ground and the furniture was practically non-existent, as was hot water. When I showered I had to gird my loins, take a deep breath and prepare myself to be doused in icy cold water. Luxurious it was not. And it still isn't. A few years ago I was in Chantilly to interview the Aga Khan on the gallops. After the interview I asked my taxi driver to stop outside what had been Pierre's yard on the Avenue de Joinville. I managed to get into the yard and found the room where I had lived for six months. The lock on the door had been broken and the door had been bashed in but it didn't look as if there had been much in the room to steal.

'You used to live here?' the taxi driver asked me in astonishment. 'You have just interviewed one of the world's richest men and yet you once lived in this!'

I agreed. And I did so in French by saying, 'oui'! When I went to France to join Pierre I didn't possess an ounce of French having hopelessly failed my French O-Level, but after a few weeks in Chantilly I began to pick up the language. When I left I wouldn't have been as fluent in the language as the likes of Edith Piaf, Charles de Gaulle or Rene Artois, but I could get by, which proved very helpful in future years when my Channel 4 guv'nor Andrew Franklin invariably asked me to interview the visiting European jockeys on amateur riders' Derby day at Epsom.

English, however, remained my first language and language was important to me then and ever since. For by the time I finished my stint in Chantilly I had decided that training racehorses, like riding them, probably wasn't for me. By this stage I knew what I wanted to be. I wanted to be a broadcaster.

THREE

HITTING THE AIRWAVES

Stanley Thompson made a tremendous success of his life. After serving his country with huge bravery during the Second World War he started a business from scratch that is still flourishing to this day. He married a wonderful woman and was a fantastic father. He truly made his mark on the world, but I cannot help but think that part of him saw in me the chance to do the things he had never quite been able to do himself.

Both Howard and I were encouraged to get involved with horses. Dad loved them and loved watching us ride, and thanks to Howard he saw one of his sons riding winners over fences. He might well have wanted us to become professional jockeys but that was a dream that could not come true. Dad might also have wanted me to become a trainer, and he clearly attempted to improve my chances by getting me jobs with Denys Smith and Pierre Sanoner, but once again the aspiration ultimately came up short. But there was another of dad's passions that I was able to take forward.

Dad was something of a performer, a bit of a showman. Brough Scott, for so long one of my Channel 4 colleagues and to this day a great friend, tells a story of how he and John Oaksey were working for ITV at Redcar during what was then the track's big summer festival, held annually around the same time that the BBC covered Glorious Goodwood. Dad started up a conversation with them both and invited them out to a restaurant that night for dinner. When they got there they found that dad had invited a sizeable number of his friends and when dinner was finished he gave a speech that must have lasted a good 20 minutes. In showbiz parlance, he was doing a turn.

Dad was at his best when he had an audience. Broadcasting gave him one. Had an interview panel picked him over David Coleman for a job at the BBC his life might have veered off in a different direction, but as the panel did not pick him, dad had to make do with the few opportunities that came his way. One was as a racing commentator. As secretary of the Cleveland point-to-point he realised that one of the most obvious things that was missing from a day at the point-to-point was a commentary. He made sure that changed. He organised the building of scaffolding in between the marquees in the middle of the course and made a vantage gantry at the top from where he relayed what was happening to grateful racegoers. Dad was the first man to commentate on a point-to-point in the north of England. Due to a decline in his health I became the youngest.

From the age of 12 I joined dad in the gantry and helped him in the role of spotter, whereby you try to give the commentator a nudge in the right direction if he has missed anything during a race. It might be whispering something in his ear or pointing at a horse who had been pulled up. Essentially it just provides the man holding the microphone with an extra pair of eyes. In one particular race that extra pair of eyes proved crucial.

It was about halfway into the three-mile contest when dad paused in the commentary, turned to me and whispered: 'I can't see them anymore.' Dad would increasingly have trouble with his eyesight as he got older and this was the first real manifestation of that decline. For a commentator there is no greater problem than not being able to see the horses. He was in real trouble.

'Will you do it for me?' he asked. I could hardly have turned him down in the circumstances, so I took hold of the microphone and finished the race for him. Then I took control of the remaining contests that afternoon and thereafter I became the local point-to-point commentator. I was only 15 at the time.

It seems a hard thing to say in the circumstances, but I loved it. Instantly I felt at home. Whereas later I would feel a sense of terror before riding in races, this was a completely comfortable experience. Alan Swinbank, now one of the north's most astute trainers, was the winning rider in what turned out to be the race that marked my commentating debut. He often reminds me of the fact. In the months and years that followed I got to commentate on plenty more of Alan's winners, but when I was commentating I had so much fun that it didn't matter to me who was winning. Except, however, for one unforgettable race at the Cleveland point-to-point.

As I've said, Howard had more success in the saddle than me, and when I was 16 I was doing the commentary in a contest that Howard was dominating from a long way out. The horse he was riding, Anna Of Siam, was trained by dad – and so effectively by me as well – which made it an even more exciting event. Going to the final fence, I got a bit carried away, and in what could have been construed as a not wholly impartial moment, shouted out in the commentary: 'Go on Howard!'

I got hauled in by the stewards for that. They were not happy.

Luckily, it in no way put a halt to my progress. Not long after my first call I wrote to Racecourse Technical Services, the body that organised the commentaries at Britain's professional race meetings. Even on major racecourses, commentaries were at that stage a relatively new innovation. It was only in 1952 that Goodwood became the first track to experiment with the novel idea of letting its customers hear what was going on. The whole thing was still pretty much in its infancy. I wrote to RTS, telling them I was commentating at point-to-points, and asked them if they would consider me for racecourse work. They said they would, but not until I was 17.

I couldn't wait for my 17th birthday to come. When it did I found that RTS had been true to their word. I was assigned a day at Market Rasen, the Lincolnshire jumps track, with Cloudesley Marsham, whose voice was heard on Britain's racecourses for many years. Cloudesley was a tremendous commentator and an equally tremendous man. He could not have been more helpful to me. First he told me to watch him at work, which I did. Then, after three of the races had been run he said I could have a go at the next two – and, I'll tell you what, during those two races I felt like I was commentating on a cloud.

RTS must have been pleased with my performance and the feedback they got from Cloudesley because they sent me a letter that offered their congratulations and the promise of work on a few days over the coming year. Again, they were true to their word, but others were also quick to offer encouragement. There was a Whit Monday when 16 meetings were taking place and RTS had a shortage of commentators. To my delight, I was called up at short notice to work at Wetherby. Among the jockeys riding that day was the man who would become one of the greatest trainers of all time, Michael Dickinson. Without me knowing it at the time, Michael wrote to RTS, told them that I had done a brilliant job and asked them to use me again. He received a nice letter back from RTS, which he still has to this day. That sort of help from such an influential figure can only have done me good. When you consider how young I was, I really couldn't have asked for more. Soon enough, though, more was coming.

After I finished my time with Pierre Sanoner in Chantilly, my main source of employment became my father. There was nothing wrong with driving the lorries for dad, and if I had done it for the rest of my life I'm sure I would have had a perfectly happy, if very different, existence, but it wasn't what I wanted to do. The chance to start earning a living doing what I did want to do came at the start of 1971.

Radio Teesside was launched by the BBC at 6pm on 31 December 1970. I dearly wanted to work in broadcasting and suddenly the BBC had started a local radio station right on my doorstep. As soon as I knew it was going to happen I wrote a letter, telling them all about me, explaining to them what I could do, offering a few ideas and asking if they might be prepared to use me. I have generally been pretty good at selling myself to others and Radio Teesside was sold on the idea of having me on the team.

One of my main suggestions had been for me to provide racing commentaries from the local meetings. In those days the world of media rights was not nearly so competitive as it is today, so it was easy enough for an organisation like Radio Teesside to send a reporter to the track. In fact for Redcar it was a win-win scenario as its meeting and sponsors got free coverage on a BBC platform. On those Saturdays when there was racing at somewhere like Redcar I would ring in to the station in the morning and do a preview of the card over the phone. Then I would head down to the station's base, where I was handed the keys to the radio car, which I drove to the track. I would then find a suitable position, raise the aerial and then stand on top of the car with my binoculars and commentate on the races, live on the radio. I should also stress, particularly to those who have questioned my attitude to money, that I did this for nothing, just as I worked for Denys Smith and Pierre Sanoner for nothing. In time I did get a little something, perhaps £2 per afternoon, but it genuinely was not the money that spurred me on. It was the desire to broadcast.

As time went on Radio Teesside – which these days is known as BBC Tees – asked me to take on other roles, such as covering some of the games at Darlington Football Club. All sports interest me so that was no hardship at all. It also helped to turn me into a more rounded sports broadcaster. And given what was about to come next for Derek Thompson, that was no bad thing at all.

FOUR

A BBC BOY

THE first I knew about the job was when I saw a notice on the wall at Radio Teesside.

'Sports News Assistant required, Broadcasting House, Sports Room, to assist with *Sports Report* and *Sport on 2*.'

That, I thought, had Tommo's name written all over it.

I should explain that by now Tommo had become my nickname and increasingly the name I used when talking to others and referring to myself. Not everyone, however, called me Tommo. To mum and dad I was always Derek. Bob Champion, who by now was plying his trade successfully as a professional jockey, always called me Derek as well, while my brother, Howard, called me then what he calls me now – Dosh. For some reason Howard seemed to develop an opinion that I was motivated mostly by money. Quite how he came to this opinion I have no idea.

Howard had joined me on a special appointment that I hoped would help me get the job. Mum, perhaps because she was a lady of some standing in the local community, decided that Howard and I should speak properly. The way to achieve this was deemed to be elocution lessons, so Howard and I were sent off to Middlesbrough for a one-hour appointment that was supposed to be split equally with me having the first 30 minutes and Howard the following half-hour. I have to admit, though, that there were not much more than ten minutes left by the time I left the elocutionist's room. What he was teaching me I found fascinating. I was keen to hone the perfect voice and this man was showing me how to do it. I was the Eliza Doolittle to his Henry Higgins and, as such, I can indeed confirm that the rain in Spain does stay mainly in the plain and that in Hartford, Hereford and Hampshire hurricanes hardly happen.

Outstanding.

The one thing about the Broadcasting House job that worried me was its location. I was a north east boy and I wanted to stay in the north east. In those days it was still a big thing for someone from my part of the country to even visit London, let alone to move there. If you told people you were going down to London they would often react as though you had named the moon as your destination. For me, it wasn't that I was frightened of moving to London – I'd survived six months in Chantilly so I was used to living in a different place – but more that I was very happy and comfortable living where I was. Even when we had gone on holiday as a family the best times had been not in far-flung places but in a caravan on the North Yorkshire coast. I adore the north of England and still go back as often as I can, staying with mum whenever possible and doing the things I did as a lad, like walking up Rosebery Topping. I knew that I wouldn't be able to do that in London.

It was also true that I couldn't work for Radio 2 in the north east and the desire to work for Radio 2 was stronger than my desire to stay in the homeland. I had to apply for the job. I did and I got an interview, which was held at Broadcasting House, the BBC's iconic Art Deco headquarters in Portland Place, a two-minute walk from Oxford Circus. Walking into the sports room for the first time was a magical moment. In those days radio was every bit as important as television and some of the top broadcasting stars were predominantly radio performers. I wanted to be one of them but first I had to impress in the interview. The main thing I was asked to do was write a preview of that day's race meeting at Sedgefield and then record it. That, pretty much, was that. I was thanked for coming and told that I would be informed of the BBC's decision in due course. All I could do was wait.

The wait proved very worthwhile. A letter arrived through the front door revealing that the job was mine if I wanted it. I did. I thought I had been successful because three of the four horses I tipped in the preview had won, but I was later told that the real reason was because they liked my style of presentation and also my voice – which showed that mum had been right to send her two sons to the elocution teacher. (It also showed that I had been right to hog most of the time.)

So it was that in 1972 I became a full-time employee of the British Broadcasting Corporation, joining the Radio 2 sports news team under the leadership of the powerful and influential Angus McKay, one of the great Scots and a true legend at the BBC. It was Angus who started the famous *Sports Report* round-up programme in 1948 and his legacy lives on as *Sports Report* continues every bit as strong today in its familiar Saturday 5pm slot. These days you can hear it on Radio 5 live, which has become the home to almost all the sport broadcast on BBC Radio. When I joined the BBC, 5 live did not even exist and Radio 2 was the station that housed most of BBC Radio's sport output, although Radio 2 had only taken over that role from Radio 3 in 1970. These were changing times, not just for me, but also for the BBC.

I had John Motson to thank for finding me a permanent place with the Beeb. Motty, a huge racing fan who almost owned part of the 1998 Grand National winner Earth Summit, had left the BBC Radio team and moved on to TV to become one of the commentators on *Match of the Day*. He had left a vacant seat at Broadcasting House and it turned out that it took two bottoms to fill it. I was not the only new member of the team. Also coming on board at the same time was Alan Parry, who went on to be another of the leading football commentators for the BBC, ITV and Sky, as well as the voice of athletics for first BBC Radio and then ITV.

In those days – and I'm pleased to report also in these days – BBC Radio was a wonderful place to work. I remember how excited I was driving south to begin my new life. Leaving home and saying goodbye to mum, dad and Howard had been pretty emotional, but everyone was delighted for me and also keen to start listening to me on the wireless. But nobody was keener than me. Enthusiasm has rarely failed me and I was positively champing at the bit to get going. Who could have blamed me? The sports room in Broadcasting House glittered with stars. I was certainly no star but I was thrilled and honoured to be joining such a superb team and such a famous organisation.

There was no doubting the identity of the number-one performer. Before Des Lynam became the face of sport on BBC Television he was the voice of sport on BBC Radio. Des, a Brighton boy, had worked his way up in a very similar way to me. At the same time the BBC started Radio Teesside they had launched a number of other local stations around the country. One of them had been Radio Brighton and Des had been snapped up. Such was his talent, Des was quickly upgraded to a national audience and the rate of his progress took him into the *Sports Report* presenter's chair in 1970 when its incumbent Peter Jones stood down to concentrate on football commentary.

Some of my early work on the sports team involved helping to write scripts for Des and assisting with the collating of news as it came in on the old teleprinters. Our output was quite prolific. As well as the flagship Saturday double-header of *Sport on 2* and *Sports Report*, we were responsible for a 15-minute bulletin that went out on week nights at 6.45pm and two-minute bulletins that were transmitted during the day at the quarter to every hour on programmes like the 'Diddy' David Hamilton show. On top of that we had slots to fill in the *Today* programme on Radio 4. There was seldom a good reason not to have something to do. And when you had Angus McKay as your boss you definitely did not want to look as though you had nothing to do. Angus, a fearsome individual, was very well aware of his own importance to BBC Radio and he protected his fiefdom with care. Angus was a radio man through and through. If anyone ever intimated they were using radio as a way of breaking into television he would eat them up and spit them out. Angus McKay's view was that if television was a bigger deal than radio he would be working in television. Which he wasn't.

One of the people able to straddle both worlds was Terry Wogan, who I got to know through working on the Angus McKay team. Terry's breakfast show included a feature called Wogan's Winner, in which Terry tipped a horse to the nation. I'll reveal a little secret here. Terry tended not to choose the horses himself. The selections came in from a team that included Laurie Brannan, who later became one of racing's best promoters as well as a long-serving journalist. But even if Terry wasn't personally responsible for Wogan's Winner he always delivered it magnificently. I learnt a lot from Terry, now, of course, Sir Terry. (If the right people are reading this, I think there's a certain ring to Sir Derek.) As well as being one of the greatest broadcasters of all time, Terry is one of the nicest men you could ever meet. When I popped my head around the corner of his studio, he would wait until a record was playing and then invite me in and we'd have a natter off air. My respect for him is vast and in some ways he was an inspiration to me. Whether he was interviewing the King of Siam or Nelly the cleaner, Terry always treated his interviewees the same. I watched what he did, and also the way in which he did it, and came to the conclusion that his way was the right way. He is also completely genuine and lacking any heirs and graces, so that if I've ever met him since he'll also make a point of saying hello and asking how I'm doing. Terry Wogan is a top man and he remains an outstanding broadcaster.

But by joining the radio sports news team I was getting to work with so many outstanding broadcasters. As well as Des and Peter Jones a personal favourite was Christopher Martin-Jenkins, who, like most of us, did a bit of everything, but in his case specialised in cricket. Our desks in room number 3096 – the room I had throughout my time at Broadcasting House – were very close to each other and Chris would often walk across and ask me in his beautiful voice: 'I say Derek, shall we have a bet today?' Chris liked a little wager now and again and was known to pop into his local betting shop when he fancied placing two shillings each-way on his personal fancy. Chris was sadly taken from us recently but so many of us have nothing but lovely memories of a lovely man.

In time Jim Rosenthal, now one of my best mates, would come on board, but no matter who else was there, Des was king and rightly so. He was also the king with the ladies, all of whom seemed to find him incredibly attractive. I experienced this at first hand on a number of occasions, including on a night out in London when the ladies were once again all fluttering eye-lashes at Des. Regrettably, the night did not pan out in the way we had hoped. Along with Bob Champion, who was in town with a few of the jockeys, we had been out at the then annual but now axed stable lads boxing championship. After watching the bouts about 20 of us went on to the Stork Club in Piccadilly. Quite a bit of champagne was drunk and at 2am it dawned on me that someone would have to pay for the fizz. The problem Des and I had was that champagne at the Stork Club was expensive, especially when put up against a BBC Radio wage. Bob had already said his goodbyes, as had plenty of the others, so while some of the other stragglers were dancing with girls I looked across at Des and said: 'Lyne, it's about time you and I made an exit.'

We had only got about 100 yards down the road when a chunky doorman came out of the club and shouted at us to stop. He let it be known that we weren't going anywhere without settling the bill.

'Lyne,' I said, 'I don't know about you, but I'm going to leg it.'

And I would have legged it had Lyne, the smooth talker that he is, not persuaded me that we should go back. Des was clearly very honest. The other explanation is that he wasn't a very good runner.

'Who's going to pay the bill?' asked the doorman.

Des looked at me. I looked at Des. The doorman looked at both of us.

'It's not us,' I said. 'Bonzo's paying.'

Bonzo, because you probably don't know, was Robin Barwell, assistant to trainer Toby Balding. The doorman accepted what I'd said and went back into the club to find Bonzo, who at that point was lying in a drunken state of collapse. He was quickly woken from it with a large doorman asking him if he was Bonzo. Sorry Bonzo. (Although I should stress that we did all later give our shares of the bill to a briefly impoverished assistant trainer.)

To everyone's great relief, not least the nation's, Des Lynam survived our night out in London and went on to become a broadcasting icon. Already an icon, and a man who would remain an icon for years to come, was Peter Bromley. Working closely with him got me out of the office and back on to racecourses, on one of which, I would make my own little piece of history.

FIVE

RED RUM, CRISP AND ME

I have been fortunate enough to witness some of the most memorable races in the sport's history but none for me has ever compared, and none ever will compare, to the Grand National of 1973. Nothing will ever come close to matching the drama, the excitement and the heroism that will always be associated with that incredible race. It was the race in which the Grand National's greatest ever winner beat the Grand National's greatest ever loser. For so many people it is the race they cherish more than any other and I have the privilege to say that I was, at least in some small way, part of it.

I had joined the BBC Radio sports news team in 1972. One year later I was part of BBC Radio's commentary team on the Grand National. I was aged only 22 and thereby became the youngest person ever to commentate on the world's most famous horserace. Unless someone tells me otherwise, I think I still am. Other people have achieved way more in their lives than me, but if I go to my grave having done no more, making that little piece of history four decades ago is enough. In fact, just having my voice associated with that special race is plenty.

When I moved down to London and took the BBC job I certainly wasn't expecting to be holding binoculars at Aintree the following year. At first, things seemed to happen very slowly only for things to then start happening very quickly. After six months I was beginning to get frustrated. It wasn't so much that I wasn't doing anything, but I was ambitious and I wasn't doing what I wanted to be doing. The biggest part of my role seemed to be behind the scenes. I was a bit like a researcher. I helped others to broadcast but seldom got the chance to broadcast myself. I collated a lot of the sports news and I wrote a lot of the sports news but I didn't get the chance to read much of the sports news. I received opportunities here and there, and during *Sport on 2* on Saturday afternoons I sometimes read the racing results, but I was like a horse who tugs hard underneath his jockey. I wanted to do more. Racing gave me the avenue to get what I wanted.

It seemed to me that racing was not covered as extensively as it might have been. We did, of course, have commentaries on all the big races from Peter Bromley but, except for the absolute showpiece racing occasions, that was that. I suggested that during *Sport on 2* at 4.55pm, five minutes before *Sports Report* started, we should have a racing round-up. After the big races of the day had been run I would frantically cut their closing stages and put together a single piece bringing them all together. Des would hand over to me and I'd say something like: 'The major race this afternoon was the Imperial Cup at Sandown. It produced a cracking finish that's well worth enjoying again. Here's how Peter Bromley saw it.'

It provided a useful link in to *Sports Report* and everyone seemed to like it. I had shown that I could be an ideas man and the decision-makers started to reward me by using me more. Best of all, I was increasingly sent out of the office. I effectively became the number-two racing man behind Peter. The racing producer, a lovely guy called John Fenton, started sending me out with Peter to whichever meeting we were covering that afternoon. This meant that almost every Saturday I was on a racecourse, as well as during the week when there was a decent race being slotted into the Radio 2 afternoon schedule. Peter would do the commentaries and I would do the rest, although if Peter ever took a week off I would stand in for him and call the horses. I loved it. I'd be lying if I said that I always enjoyed working with Peter but it was an honour to do so.

In my eyes, two racing commentators stand head and shoulders above the rest. With no disrespect to those behind them, Peter O'Sullevan and Peter Bromley lead the field by a mile. And, in my own opinion, Peter Bromley's description of the 1973 Grand National finish is not just the best racing commentary of all time but the best sporting commentary of all time. It really was outstanding. It came 13 years after Peter had been made the BBC's first specialist sports correspondent. When he retired immediately after calling home Galileo in the 2001 Derby he had put his voice to exactly 200 Classics and more than 10,000 races. As a commentator he knew that his job was far more than just repeatedly running through the order in which the horses were running. He knew he had to paint a picture of a race – especially important, of course, as his audience were listening on what he always called the wireless and could therefore not see the action. Like Peter O'Sullevan, he had a wonderfully distinctive voice and when he got towards the end of a race his gravelly tones really hit a fever pitch, in the same way that BBC Radio's current lead commentator, the superb John Hunt, does today. Peter could certainly go through the decibels in a tight finish. He could do the same when he got angry.

I'm not sure Peter Bromley liked me, and I'm not sure I necessarily liked him, but I respected him hugely. Peter could be ferocious and frightening. If something or someone had annoyed him the displeasure boomed out of his body. He felt he had right on his side, he knew he was good and he demanded obedience and adherence. On occasions he was extremely kind to me, such as the day he invited me into his home near Reading and I met his family, but he was also the sort of person you walked around on tiptoes. He was from the old school and I was from the new school – and the gap between the two schools back then was gigantic. Peter saw nothing wrong in shouting at those he considered junior to him. I very much fell into that bracket. I got a verbal bashing from him on more than one occasion. They could be upsetting, so much so that Peter once made me cry.

The fault was mine. Peter always liked to set off home as soon as his work was done. It was almost unheard of for the last race on a card to be covered by Radio 2 as the best contests were almost always earlier in the day. On the very biggest days Peter would sometimes have to hang around a little longer so that the programme could go back to him for some live reflections on the afternoon. This always happened on Derby Day. I think we came off air at 4.30pm. I must have agreed to see Peter after we finished to do something or other – I can't remember what – but I was also particularly keen to say hello to a few friends who had spent the day at Epsom. I must have got to Peter 15 or 20 minutes late, not really thinking that on Derby Day he would be desperate to leave. I was wrong and when I got to him he looked at me with a face like thunder and shouted at me like a stern parent telling off a child. It reduced me to tears.

But although Peter was maybe not the gentlest man in the world, he was an exceptional commentator and it was my great blessing that I was given the chance to work with him. From 1973 to 1980 I also got the chance to commentate on the same race, the greatest of all races, with him. The first time was the best of all.

Among my colleagues for *Sport on 2*'s coverage of the 1973 Grand National were Peter Bromley, Michael Seth-Smith, Michael O'Hehir, Des Lynam and Judith Chalmers.

Judith, who, of course, became famous presenting the holiday programme *Wish You Were Here?*, would never have claimed to be a racing expert, and you would not have expected to see her at Donny on Lincoln day, but she was a fine addition to the team for events like the Grand National. Judith did a lot of the colourful, scene-setting pieces, but at no point did she need to hold a pair of binoculars. The only ones that had to do that were Peter, the two Michaels and myself.

Quite obviously, Peter had the honour of doing his stint from the grandstand with his three colleagues positioned out in the country. The hardest job of all was probably given to Michael Seth-Smith. Only people of a certain age will now remember Michael, and because he did not really do a great deal of TV, it's not easy to find recordings with his voice on, but it was beautiful and creamy. He was the number-one racecourse commentator of his time, so if you were at the races at, say, Ascot or Cheltenham, it was Michael you would have heard. For the Grand National he was based down at the first fence, so it was Michael who had to keep an eye out for any fallers. With sometimes more than 40 horses to cover in those days that was no easy task.

Michael sounded like the text-book Englishman. After taking the field over the fourth fence he would hand over to someone who was the ultimate Irishman. Michael O'Hehir was a super-star at home. Everyone in Ireland knew his name and, more importantly, everyone in Ireland knew his voice. Michael was possibly the most famous and best-loved sports broadcaster that his country has ever produced. He was known as the voice of Gaelic games and he commentated on all the major horser-aces, but he was also used on major non-sporting occasions, including when famously talking over John F Kennedy's funeral for five consecutive hours. Yet nothing Michael did is as well known as his description of the 'right pile-up' that occurred at the 23rd fence of the 1967 Grand National, one of 25 Grand National commentaries he did for the BBC, some for television, some for radio. It was because Michael, as usual, had been to the weighing room before the race that he learnt John Buckingham was wearing different colours to those he was supposed to don on 100-1 outsider Foinavon. Michael was therefore able to pick out Foinavon clambering over the fence and then continuing on his way to the most unlikely Aintree triumph.

In 1973 Michael was part of the BBC Radio team and was in his usual spot at Becher's Brook. Michael always used to call me Mr Thomp-son, carefully splitting the two syllables in my surname, which never failed to make me chuckle. On Grand

National day Michael would get a lift in a police car down to his commentary box. I would come along with him in the car and smile as Michael waved to racegoers on the way, shouting at them: 'Enjoy yourselves!' When we got to Becher's Michael would get out and I remember the policeman saying to me in my first year: 'Right son, where do you want me to drop you off?' 'Just around the corner,' I said. It was marvellous.

For me, my Grand National home was the fence after Valentine's Brook. Michael would hand over to me just after the leaders had landed at Valentine's and I would then pick up the commentary and describe the action over the next three fences until handing back to Peter Bromley as the field galloped across the Melling Road and on to the racecourse proper. It was a bit surreal but completely wonderful. I was what felt like miles away from the grandstand. People tended to congregate near where the two Michaels were based but I was practically alone except for John Hanmer, who always called the race from the same area for BBC Television.

As I got inside the box on that Saturday afternoon on 31 March 1973, it did feel like a turning point in my life. It had been my ambition to commentate on the race ever since dad took me to the National for the first time ten years earlier. Now I had made it. Working on the National is the ultimate accolade for any racing commentator. I haven't done it since 1980 and I still miss it. For horses, jockeys and commentators it is the hardest race in the world. For most of the years after I finished working on the race for BBC Radio I would still listen to the race on BBC Radio because I would have been at one of the afternoon's other meetings, perhaps Hereford, Newcastle or Lingfield, working for ITV and then Channel 4. We would always finish early – we knew everybody was watching what the BBC was doing from Aintree so it was hardly worth us doing a programme at all – and so I was able to enjoy the radio coverage while driving home. Whenever I did I could hear in the voices of the commentators what was in my voice on that day in 1973 – unparalleled excitement. The Grand National is different. It is a race like no other, but it is also a race that has an audience far bigger than for anything else we do. You always know how important it is to get it right. You need to concentrate 150 per cent. Concentrating 100 per cent just isn't enough.

For me it was slightly easier. By the time they got to me for the first time, the field had already thinned out a bit, second time round even more so. And in my first National I had no trouble spotting the leader. As the race entered my territory, and I had the honour of hearing Michael O'Hehir hand over to me for the first time, Crisp was clearly out in front. An Australian import, he had showed himself to be a top-class chaser. In 1971 he won the Champion Chase over two miles by 25 lengths. In 1972 he took fourth in the Cheltenham Gold Cup before dropping back in distance in 1973 to finish third in the Champion Chase. Speed was his forte, as was his jumping, which was bold and breathtaking. Both would be in his favour at Aintree, but against him was the fact that he had to carry top weight of 12st – 23lb more than Red Rum had on his back – and he was far from certain to stay the gruelling four-and-a-half-mile journey. To make his life even more difficult, trainer Fred Winter and jockey Richard Pitman felt they had to let him adopt his customary front-running role. If Crisp was going to win the Grand National he would have to do it the hard way.

But you could argue that the same was true of Red Rum. The horse I had seen at Wetherby with the gorgeous stable girl a few years earlier had subsequently moved to Southport to join the yard of Ginger McCain. I had seen him there myself as we had done some pieces on the horse in the build-up to the race. It had been worth doing so because he was one of the leading fancies – he was sent off 9-1 joint-favourite with Crisp – but he was also at the centre of a romantic tale. He was the horse trained from a second-hand car showroom by a taxi driver who often exercised his best horse on the beach. If Red Rum could win the Grand National he would make for a superb story. At the time we didn't know just how superb.

As Michael handed over to me I got a little over-excited and some of the first words I said were: 'Three fences have fallen at that horse.' Happily I can report that I got better and more relaxed as the race went on. As everyone now knows, Crisp opened up a lead of unprecedented proportions, one that increased when his nearest pursuer Grey Sombrero fell at the Chair. As he began his second circuit Michael Seth-Smith said: 'I have never seen in all my Nationals a horse so far ahead. He is over 20 lengths ahead.' Then as Michael O'Hehir watched the action at Becher's Brook he said: 'Crisp is almost a fence in front. He is skipping over these fences as if they were hurdles. He is 25 lengths in front with Red Rum in hot pursuit.'

Then it was my turn again. Michael O'Hehir had been right. Crisp was almost a fence in front. In fact as he jumped the 26th fence right in front of me, I could see that a number of the runners were still jumping the Canal Turn, two fences further back. At that point I announced that the distance between

51

Crisp and Richard Pitman and Red Rum and Brian Fletcher was 20 lengths, but I could see the lead was being nibbled into. As Crisp went back across the Melling Road, Richard Pitman was starting to really push Crisp for the first time. The distress signals were starting to come out. Brian Fletcher could sense that. He gave Rummy a smack across the backside to urge him on.

I said: 'Crisp is 20 lengths in front but Red Rum is reducing the lead to 15 lengths.' And then, for the first time in my career, and aged only 22, I told the world – for the Grand National commentary was played out on the BBC World Service – that Peter Bromley would now describe the finish of the National.

And it was the perfect description. Some of the best advice Peter ever gave me was to try to identify the likely winner with two furlongs to run. Peter identified that Crisp was running on empty and that Red Rum was catching him. Here is what he said:

'As they come to the Elbow now, Crisp is under pressure. He doesn't know where he's going. Richard Pitman is trying to keep him going. Red Rum is closing the gap. Defeat is facing him as Crisp has 200 yards to run and the National isn't over yet. Crisp is keeping going. It's going to be a desperately near thing, but Crisp is walking. Twenty-five yards to go. Red Rum goes sailing past to snatch the National. Crisp is second and the rest don't matter, for we will never see another race like that in a hundred years.'

You cannot better that.

'Defeat is facing him' and 'Red Rum goes sailing past to snatch the National' painted the picture as vividly as it could possibly have been painted, but then, in the heat of the moment, to sum up what he had just seen with those immortal words, 'we will never see another race like that in a hundred years', was beyond outstanding. And I had the privilege of being part of the commentary in which he said it. My voice is on it forever. It's something nobody can ever take away from me and even now, as I write these words 40 years later, it's one of the things about which I feel the most proud.

I hope that 40 years later Richard Pitman also feels proud for having being involved in one of jumping's defining races. Richard was the first to admit that he got things wrong on Crisp and made mistakes that, had they not been made, might well have resulted in Crisp winning the Grand National. But so what? Every single one of us makes mistakes. In Richard's case his main error was in persisting with his use of the whip in the right hand when his mount was drifting badly left and therefore off the true racing line and towards the Chair. Richard knows he got that wrong but for the rest of the race he had got it absolutely right. And how many of us, having made a mistake like that in front of hundreds of millions of people worldwide, would so quickly have admitted our guilt without the merest attempt to deflect even a smidgeon of blame to either another person or to circumstance? I've met a lot of fine people over the years but few have been finer than Rich. He made many friends that afternoon, and although he didn't come away as a Grand National winner, he did not return to Lambourn totally empty-handed.

Peter Bromley made sure he went home with something that was not quite the same as a winner's trophy but good to have nonetheless. Throughout his commentating career Peter used a little rubber stamp that when pressed on to paper showed the outline of a jockey. On his personal racecard he would impress it against the name of every horse and then colour in the silks, so he could identify all the runners. He did this so beautifully that, when framed, it would be worthy of a place on anyone's wall, and after every Grand National he would present his colour chart to the winning jockey. After the 1973 race, having decided that this was really Crisp's Grand National, he gave his chart not to Red Rum's rider Brian Fletcher but to Richard Pitman. It was a lovely thing to do.

Sadly for Rich, he would never gain Grand National compensation. Just like the Gold Cup, which he came so agonisingly close to winning on Pendil, the world's greatest steeplechase eluded him, but he remained involved in the race for decades afterwards as a pundit for BBC Television. For Red Rum, however, the story was far from over. He returned to Aintree, and I returned as well, over the next four years, winning under Brian in 1974 before finishing second in 1975 (again with Brian on board) before once more taking the runner-up spot in 1976, by which point Ginger McCain had replaced Brian with Tommy Stack. But in 1977 immortality belonged to Rummy as he came home clear of Churchtown Boy to claim his third Grand National.

Throughout his era I was a regular visitor to his and Ginger's home. Radio 2 went down there on an annual basis and we produced some fantastic features following him. It was the sort of story Hollywood would have turned down for being unbelievable. He was an amazing horse but he had an amazing trainer. Ginger's poor wife Beryl had to cope with him for all those years, which I'm sure wasn't easy, but for those of us who didn't have to live with Ginger he was a joy. He was so natural, so normal and so different to those trainers who have an inflated idea of their own talent and importance. Some of those trainers are not nearly as good as they think they are. Some are sent incredible raw material and train from some of the plushest facilities money can buy, yet they still manage to regularly mess things up. Not so Ginger. He trained from the back of a car showroom and worked mainly at the lower end of the sport but he managed to mastermind the career of a racehorse whose name will live on forever. It's fitting that Aintree now has an incredibly lifelike sculpture of Ginger overlooking the new winner's enclosure, which he must have been so proud to enter alongside his son and successor Donald after Ballabriggs followed up the victories of Red Rum and Amberleigh House for the McCain family.

Sadly I wasn't there to see Amberleigh House or Ballabriggs win as Channel 4 commitments prevented me from going. Now those commitments don't exist and I returned to Aintree in 2013, 33 years after I commentated on the race for the last time for BBC Radio, and exactly forty years after I stood by the fence after Valentine's Brook for the first time. I was still four months short of my 23rd birthday that day. There were still seven Grand Nationals and eight more years with the BBC ahead of me, but nothing in those eight years could ever have matched what I saw when Red Rum met Crisp. In truth, nothing in the 40 years that followed ever has. Even as a young man, I don't suppose I expected it to.

For all of us who were there that afternoon, the National of 1973 was as good as it gets.

SIX

ITCHY FEET

Perhaps I should have mentioned before now that I had not been spending my life alone. Not long after I moved from the north east to London I was joined by the girl who had become my steady girlfriend, Jenny Colley. Not long after the 1973 Grand National we became man and wife. Jenny was the first of what has turned out to be three Mrs J Thompsons. In total, I have been married to a Jenny, a Janie and a Julie. With that history behind me I've told Johnny Francome that if I ever start getting flirtatious he should be on his guard.

I should never have married Jenny and I'm sure she feels the same. We didn't use the words at the time, but we could easily have looked each other in the eye and said: 'It's not you, it's me.' Neither of us was ready to be married. I was very young and very naive. I should also have stayed very single.

Jenny was a pretty blonde-haired lady who worked at Radio Teesside. She was lovely and a smashing girlfriend but I should never have allowed myself to get into the situation where she became my wife. The problem was that it was all too easy. I liked the idea of having a partner – although I also liked the idea of not having a partner – and Jenny was keen to advance her career in London. She moved down to the capital a few months after me and we spent a lot of time together in one of the Hyde Park apartments the BBC rented out to employees who had just joined from other parts of the country. Jenny also made the switch from Radio Teesside to Radio 2 and landed a job as a producer, at which she was an enormous success.

Jenny, the daughter of a headmaster and a couple of years older than me, was from Doncaster, and it was in Doncaster that we got married. For all I know, Jenny's friends were telling her what my friends were telling me. 'Don't do it!' In the early 1970s, however, people did do it. If you were going to cohabit you tended to take the next step and get married. Mum was happy to go along with the plan, but my mates in the BBC sports room tried to talk me out of it. So did Bob Champion and so did dad. They knew I was too young and they knew I was making a mistake. As I stood at the altar during what was a very nice, and not inexpensive, wedding day, so did I. In theory I could have put a halt to proceedings there and then, but I didn't have the courage to let everybody down. 'Tommo,' I thought. 'You've got this one very badly wrong.' Even so, I still said: 'I do.'

Our first proper marital home together was a lovely flat in Westminster that cost £12 a week to rent. In today's money you would get £2,000 a week for it. We decided to leave Westminster because we wanted to buy and could never have afforded a place there. We moved out and rented cheaper properties in Surrey before buying a little house in Walton on Thames, slap bang between Sandown and Kempton. Both of us were still working at the BBC, but apart from that the only thing that joined us together was a shared surname. When we socialised we did so separately and with our own friends. We lived our own lives. It was obvious to both of us that we should never have got hitched, but that at least made it easier to rectify the situation. After three years of marriage we divorced. It wasn't in the least bit acrimonious and in some ways our marriage was not actually a mistake because neither of us really got hurt. We did not have any children together so nobody else had been scarred by our actions. We had been effectively living apart while living together, which meant that after the marriage ended very little changed.

I regret to say that we did not stay friends, not because we hated each other, but because we did not bother to make the effort. At least I know I didn't. It's a reflection on my failings that I do not have many memories of my time together with Jenny. She was another example of me pushing to the back of my mind something I did not want to have at the front of my mind. We had some good times together but too many of those good times occurred when we were not in each other's company. I remember, for example, that when we were courting I would always stay with Jenny and her family if I was working at Doncaster. During that time I became friends with the bloodstock agent Peter Doyle, who now buys many of Richard Hannon's horses. At first I was mates with Peter's dad, Jack, an even more legendary bloodstock agent who I always addressed as Uncle Jack. It was Jack who introduced me to Peter and we had some good nights out. One evening Peter came around to Jenny's family's house and we stayed up until late playing cards. The game of choice was three card brag, in which you get dealt three cards each and bet on what you have in your hand. To have three of a kind is the ultimate aim. Peter drew one seven and then another seven. Nobody I knew had ever drawn three sevens so I told him that if he drew another I would give him £20, which these days would have been the equivalent of about £200. He drew another seven.

I was devastated.

He still asks me if I remember the day he pulled out three sevens? He knows very well that I'll never forget it.

Peter remains a good pal but I know nothing about the whereabouts of Jenny. I presume she remarried, had children and has had a good life but that's only an assumption. I haven't seen her for 25 years. Plenty of people who know me do not even know that Jenny existed. She did exist, but in my head it's almost as if she did not. That is in no way a reflection on Jenny. It's a reflection on me.

It would be wrong to say the end of my marriage to Jenny did not have an effect on me. Subconsciously it did, and the effect was not good. I had never been a pipe and slippers man, and I've always enjoyed a good night out, but I started to enjoy a few too many good nights. I hadn't exactly been chained to the house when married to Jenny, so in one sense my circumstances had not changed a great deal, but I seemed to want to make the most of once again being officially a free agent. There was many an evening in town, lots of alcohol, numerous parties and the odd woman. Not surprisingly, that all had an impact on my work.

It first materialised one afternoon when I was due to be reading out the racing results. I couldn't. I got into the studio, got myself sat down and realised immediately something was not right. This sounds odd, but I felt breathless without actually being short of breath. It was the strangest sensation. Just as worrying, I felt nervous. It was almost as though I was experiencing a touch of stage fright. 'Gee, what's going on here?', I thought to myself. I got through it and tried to put what had happened to the back of my mind, in the way I like to do, but I was unable to put it to the back of my mind for long because it soon happened again. This time it was on the overnight shift that we had to do once a week. The shift ended with the reading of bulletins at 7.25am and 8.25am in Radio 4's *Today* programme. Once again, I couldn't do it. The studio assistant told me to compose myself but it didn't seem to make any difference.

I could see something was wrong with me, people at work could see something was wrong with me and even dad, all those miles away back home, could see the same. He wrote me a letter. It was obvious he was concerned. He told me I was spending too much time going out at night in London. He told me I wasn't spending enough time in my own bed and he told me I wasn't getting enough sleep. He told me I had to show more dedication to the job and I knew he was right.

To tide me over the worst part, I asked at work if, for a while at least, I could concentrate on production rather than presenting. They agreed to this but, like dad, they advised me to see a doctor. I ended up seeing more than one. I explained my symptoms to one and after a long conversation he advised me to try drinking more water. What a genius! Nothing anybody suggested seemed to help, but then just at the point when I was starting to get really worried, I heeded the recommendation of a friend and went to a doctor in London's Harley Street. I explained to him in detail what was wrong and asked him if he thought he could help.

'Yes, of course,' he said and prescribed me some pills, which he said I should start using. The following day I started taking Beta blockers, a medication on occasions given to people like myself that were showing symptoms similar to those associated with hypertension. For the next two years I was a regular user and in the early months of taking them I'm sure they did help me, even if only psychologically.

Increasingly, though, I felt my broadcasting career needed help in other areas. More and more I started to feel frustrated at BBC Radio. There was nothing wrong with the job I had, but my feet had begun to itch. Professionally I was given opportunities and I continued as number-two racing commentator to Peter Bromley as well as his sidekick at racecourses. When Peter was on holiday I stood in for him, as I did if Peter was ever taken ill at short notice. More than once Peter fell ill the night before one of the big sprint handicaps, races that were contested by 30 runners. One of those occasions was the night before the 1978 Stewards' Cup.

'Tommo, Peter's ill, you're doing the Stewards' Cup,' was the message in the phone call at 10pm on the night before the race, and so it was that it was not Peter's voice but mine that described future sprinting star Ahonoora winning the Glorious Goodwood dash at 50-1.

As well as doing the racing work, I read bulletins on Radio 2 and Radio 4 and occasionally got to present *Sport on 2* when Des Lynam was not available. That was an honour but it was an honour that came along all too rarely. I also got to meet some very well known people and I once spent three hours on a Sunday evening with tennis legend Fred Perry, who had come to Broadcasting House to record an interview prior to the US

Open and ended up hanging around because he was enjoying himself.

George Harrison did not even have an excuse to be there. I walked into the sports room one Sunday afternoon and there he was, a Beatle sat on a chair at my desk watching a grand prix. I looked at him, reality registered and I said: 'You're George Harrison.' He agreed he was indeed George Harrison and explained that he had come in specifically to watch the grand prix. He loved motor racing and knew that he would be able to watch our feed of a race was not being shown live on television. That was an afternoon to remember.

Another afternoon I won't forget was the one for BBC Radio at Epsom on Derby Day when Tommy Steele gave one of the best interviews of my career. He told me how much the Derby meant to him and how as a Cockney lad he used to come to the Downs and watch the Derby from near Tattenham Corner. He said the school gave the children the day off for the Derby – imagine that happening now – and made it crystal clear how much he loved going. Even when he was all grown up Tommy did not physically grow very far, but as a young boy he was even smaller, so he used to run through people's legs to find a place against the rail to see the Classic field gallop past him.

'All I could see was the horses briefly thunder past me,' he said. 'Whoosh. Then they were gone. Three seconds and it was all over for another year. But I've never forgotten what it was like. Never.'

On days like that the job was a joy, but as I entered my ninth year in the post it was no longer enough. When jobs came up and I thought other people were better suited to them than me, I was happy for them to get the job. People who were progressing better than I was deserved to be recognised. I had no complaints with that whatsoever. Yet when people who I thought were less talented than me climbed up the ladder while I remained in the same place I began to get thoroughly fed up.

The job no longer satisfied me and the money definitely did not. I was on £12,000 a year, not in itself a bad salary by any means, but I was sure I could do better. I was constantly over-drawn at the bank and constantly struggling to make ends meet. I would walk down Regent Street and see all the Mercedes-Benz and BMW cars on the road and think that the cars cost more than I was earning after tax in a whole year. How was that possible? Why couldn't I afford a car like that? And as I couldn't afford a car like that, what could I do to change things?

The answer was ITV.

SEVEN

TOMMO'S ON THE TELLY

I f it had not been for Bob Champion I might never have made it on to television. I might have stayed with BBC Radio, feeling a bit sorry for myself and waiting for opportunities that may or may not have arrived. Instead I got a phone call from my best friend that turned my life in a very different direction.

'Have you applied for the job yet?' Bob asked me.

'What job?' I asked back.

'The ITV job?'

'What ITV job?'

I genuinely knew nothing about it. Ken Butler, who had been ITV's principal paddock commentator for years, was retiring and ITV planned to replace him. Apparently it was widely known on racecourses but the news had got nowhere near to reaching my ear.

'You've got to go for it,' Bob told me. He reckoned I was made for it. Perhaps I was. I wasn't necessarily sure. A paddock role seemed to me likely to involve a lot of form summarising that was not necessarily my strength. But although it might not on paper have been my perfect TV racing job, it was a TV racing job,

65

a new job, a new chance and an opportunity to break into the world of television. I had literally never done anything in front of a camera. I would not be able to offer them any experience but I could offer them Tommo. I hoped Tommo would be enough.

Bob passed on the information exactly a week before the interviews were due to take place at Sandown. I knew some of the ITV guys from my racing work for Radio 2, so I asked the right people if I could be seen at Sandown. They agreed. I was a runner in the race. Now I had to get fit.

For the next week Champ (Bob Champion) and I were like two schoolboys before an exam, frantically revising for a test that could change my life. I thought long and hard about what questions they would ask me. I came up with what must have been at least 50 possible questions and I rehearsed at least 50 possible answers. When Champ thought my answer wasn't as it should have been, he told me and advised what he thought I should say instead. He worked long and hard to give me the best possible chance of getting the gig.

The gig I was going for would definitely move me a few rungs up the career ladder. The majority of ITV's racing coverage appeared in the Saturday afternoon show, *World of Sport*, but there were midweek meetings covered as well. Racing was one of ITV's most regularly shown sports, so appointing the right person was deemed to be important. Among those making the decision were ITV's head of sport John Bromley and his number two Bob Burrows, who had been one of Angus McKay's main men on the BBC Radio sport team before doing what Angus would have considered unthinkable and moving across to the dark side, namely television. It was a move I was hoping to make as well, and I was no less enthusiastic after my performance at Sandown on the Friday of the Tingle Creek Chase meeting in early December 1980.

I went home with hope in my heart. By now I dearly wanted to be part of the ITV racing team. I was desperate to hear good news. Early one morning, the good news came. It was John Bromley on the phone. I was being offered a job but not the job for which I had applied. The paddock commentator's role had gone to Jim McGrath, who, with his Timeform credentials, was undeniably better suited to the post. I had lost out to Jim but John explained that they had been impressed by me and wanted me on board as a presenter and reporter. I was thrilled. They wanted me so much that they were effectively creating a new job to accommodate me. It was only towards the end of the conversation that I even thought about money. (Honestly.) I asked how much I would be paid. The answer was £7,500 per year.

Ouch.

That represented a pay cut of nearly 40 per cent. I asked John if there was any flexibility on the money front. He said there wasn't but added that, unlike the BBC, ITV would not limit me in what I could do and, where it was felt appropriate, I could work for others as well.

I did not accept the offer there and then, purely because the income drop worried me. One of the reasons I had been looking to leave the BBC was because I felt I was not earning what I should have been earning. By going to ITV I would end up earning even less. The only course of action I had open to me was to let the BBC know what was happening. I told them I had been offered a job presenting racing on *World of Sport*. When that news had sunk in I was made to feel wanted by the BBC for the first time in years. They assured me they wanted me to stay. They offered me this and they offered me that. Suddenly I felt in a strong bargaining position.

I told them I wanted Peter Bromley's job.

'Give me that and I'll stay,' I said.

My thought at the time was that Peter might not be far off wanting to retire – I was wrong because he stayed on until 2001 – and I reckoned I had nothing to lose by attempting to muscle in on his commentary box. The BBC came back to me and promised to almost double my salary and give me more presenting opportunities. They could not, however, give me Peter Bromley's job because they said Peter Bromley was still there and to their knowledge had no plans to quit. I now knew where I stood. I could go to ITV and work on racing for £7,500 a year with the possible option of taking other work in addition, or I could stay on the BBC Radio sport team for a significantly boosted salary of more than £20,000 a year.

I told the BBC not to worry. I explained to them that I loved racing and that I would therefore accept ITV's offer. I was leaving the BBC and leaving radio. Television beckoned.

By joining *World of Sport* I was not only leaving the BBC but I was taking on a BBC institution.

World of Sport had been launched in 1965 as a rival to the BBC's Grandstand and by the time I joined it had long since developed its own identity. Nobody at *World of Sport* would have denied that the BBC had the majority of the good stuff. Aside from racing, *World of Sport*'s most frequently covered sport was British wrestling. The joke in TV circles at the time was that the BBC had gone through the alphabet and bought up the rights to all the showpiece sports. By the time they arrived at the letter 'w' all the money had been spent. Sometimes, however, a sport had divided up its rights between the BBC and ITV, racing being one of them. When I moved across, BBC Television still showed around 100 days of racing a year with a portfolio that included Ascot, Aintree, Cheltenham, Goodwood and Newbury. ITV, however, were anything but small-time players in the racing world. Their racecourses included Epsom (which meant ITV had the Derby), Newmarket (which gave ITV both of the Guineas), Sandown, Doncaster, York and Kempton, which had just moved to ITV from the BBC. Some racecourses, such as Haydock, Lingfield and Chepstow, had deals with the BBC whereby the BBC had the first pick of their meetings with ITV then having the option of mopping up what was left. The BBC might have had most of racing's crown jewels but we had plenty of our own and more than enough racing rights to showcase the sport nearly every Saturday of the year.

World of Sport traditionally opened with a football slot hosted by Ian St John and Jimmy Greaves, while once a year almost the entire show was given over to the FA Cup Final. We increasingly did a lot of snooker, while speedway, cycling, hockey, showjumping, bowls, ice skating and darts all made regular appearances, as occasionally did golf. Sometimes, though, the nearly five-hour programme was harder to fill and viewers often got to see sports that very seldom had a chance of finding air time elsewhere, sports such as polo, at which I sometimes acted as an interviewer, badminton, table tennis and yachting. Even more obscure sports were sometimes given a slot, with stock car racing and even rock climbing making the occasional appearance. Fortunately, I never had to scale a mountain.

Racing was very much my main duty on *World of Sport* and the racing team I was joining was pretty special. At its helm was the main presenter Brough Scott and his most senior colleague, John Oaksey, both of them former jockeys. Both were also fantastic men. In the sometimes selfish world of television either man could have sought to make life difficult for me but they could not have been more welcoming.

I remember seeing Brough ride a winner when dad and I once went south to watch a meeting at Sandown. At that stage I wouldn't have been expecting to one day work with him. After he left the weighing room Brough quickly established himself as one of racing's top writers and broadcasters, and by the time I became a colleague he had been working with ITV for a decade. As the main presenter of ITV's racing coverage, and then Channel 4's, Brough was exceptional, bringing style, gravitas and intelligence to the role, not to mention an insider's knowledge.

John Oaksey also had that same inside knowledge. He had been one of the finest amateur riders in the history of the sport, winning the Hennessy Gold Cup, Whitbread Gold Cup and so nearly also the Grand National when second on Carrickbeg in 1963. John, or Oaks as I called him, had been on ITV since 1969, but carried on riding until 1975 and famously founded the Injured Jockeys Fund. He was the toughest guy I've ever met and also the most accomplished and entertaining after-dinner speaker I've ever heard. He was also one of the tightest people I've come across. People call me careful with money but Oaks was even worse and nicked my copy of *The Sporting Life* and then *Racing Post* on countless occasions.

Brough and John led the ITV team, but as well as Jim McGrath and myself, we also had three regular commentators, headed up by Graham Goode, who in 1981, my debut ITV year, had been appointed lead caller for the first time. John Penney and Raleigh Gilbert, who had shared the number-one spot for most of the 1970s, remained on board and continued to get lots of work because we covered lots of meetings, while John Tyrrell, known to us all as JT, voiced over betting and results. John McCririck would later come on board as the betting expert, and as ITV racing morphed into Channel 4 racing the team would get much bigger still, but back then we were a small and, I'd like to think, quite select band.

Anchoring the whole *World of Sport* show was Dickie Davies, a man for whom I had a tremendous amount of respect. Dickie had taken over as *World of Sport*'s principal presenter in 1968 when Eamonn Andrews left the show. A supreme professional, he was as inextricably linked with *World of Sport* as was the programme's famous theme tune. He was a lovely guy. I'd met him before joining ITV at the odd sporting event. The thought that Dickie Davies would soon be introducing Derek Thompson felt like a seriously big deal to me.

The deal was done for the first time at Ayr on a late Saturday in January 1981. I took on a role that day that became familiar to me over the next four years, that of second site presenter – and on *World of Sport* there was invariably a second site. In an attempt to make the programme more enticing to viewers ITV tried, where possible, to offer seven races during the afternoon, or at the very least six. To run alongside the races ITV and bookmakers promoted an accumulator bet called the ITV Seven or ITV Six depending on the number of races we were televising.

(On the rare occasions when we had only one meeting it was the ITV Three or ITV Four.) The bet helped racing become a real cornerstone of ITV's Saturday afternoon schedules and it also meant that our second racecourse, although sometimes of little consequence as a race meeting in itself, took on greater importance. Knowing that, *World of Sport*'s producers always sent a presenter to the number-two meeting, something that generally doesn't happen now on Channel 4. That someone became me. So while Brough or John – or sometimes Brough accompanied by John or Jim McGrath – would have gone to Sandown for four races on Eclipse day, I would have been sent to Haydock to cover three races headed by the Lancashire Oaks and Old Newton Cup. Or if the main men were at Newmarket for the Champion Stakes, I would have been at Kempton for the Charisma Gold Cup. Very often the support act was not as enticing as that. I spent quite a few *World of Sport* Saturdays at the likes of Catterick, Wolverhampton, Market Rasen or back home at Redcar. That did not bother me in the slightest. In fact, I think doing meetings like that was really important in the building of my profile and popularity. It was from doing those days that I seemed to attract a bit of a following and it was also from doing those days that I got in touch with real people who love their racing. It was then that Tommo was truly born.

As I've said before, some of my friends had been calling me Tommo for ages, but Tommo had never existed on the BBC. Whenever I was working on Radio 2 or Radio 4 I was always Derek Thompson while on air. Even when I returned to the BBC for the 2013 Cheltenham Festival it was made clear that I would be known as Derek, not Tommo – although that was easier said than done. *World of Sport*, although completely professional, maybe had a lighter feel to it than the BBC's Grandstand, and there was never any problem with me being referred to as Tommo when it seemed natural and appropriate. I loved it. My job is to entertain people and to make their racing experience – whether they are on a racecourse, watching at home or listening on the radio – more enjoyable than it would have been without me. If by calling me Tommo I seem accessible, normal and one of them, and it therefore becomes easier for them to interact with me and feel comfortable with me, then so much the better.

For my first *World of Sport* shift at Ayr I was accompanied by Mark Jackson, one of the main producers. Mark had come along to give me support and hold my hand on my big day. Being accompanied by anyone turned out to be a novel experience. Doing racing for *World of Sport* could be a pretty lonely existence. Whereas now I like to take my microphone around the racecourse, speaking to anybody who wants to speak to me, and sometimes to people who it transpires don't want to speak to me, on those ITV Saturdays I was in a fixed position. Regardless of where you were at, the presenter was positioned sat behind a desk in a small studio branded with ITV Sport livery. The entire broadcast was spent there. There was no wandering around the track searching for potential interviewees. We did not even go into the winner's enclosure to do post-race interviews, or I certainly did not. Brough might occasionally have done that at the bigger meetings, but for the fixtures I worked on there was no need. It was an understandable decision.

If you take, as an example, this running order from 21 November 1981, you can see how much we had to fit in:

1.25   ITV Six. Racing from Ayr (presented by Brough Scott, commentary from Graham Goode) and Catterick (presented by Derek Thompson, commentary by Raleigh Gilbert)

1.30   Ayr: Panama Cigar Hurdle (Series Qualifier) 2m

1.45   Catterick: Cocked Hat Farm Foods Novices' Chase (3m½f)

2.00   Ayr: Bass Special Handicap Chase (2m4f)

2.05:   Back to Dickie Davies in studio for the latest Saturday football team news.

2.15   Catterick: State Express Young Steeplechasers' Qualifier Novice Chase (2m)

2.30   Ayr: John Mackay Handicap Chase (3m½f)

2.45   Catterick: William Hill Handicap Hurdle (2m)

2.55   Back to Dickie Davies in studio

That represented a lot of racing, and a lot of television, in not a lot of time, especially during the jumps season when the races took longer to run. Within that 90-minute window we not only had to accommodate a link back to Dickie – and sometimes there was more than one link if it was felt that something of particular importance needed to be passed on to the viewers – but also a number of commercial breaks. Clearly we were in competition with *Grandstand* and if a story broke ITV wanted to break it before the BBC. That meant returning to Catterick sometimes had to be delayed. It was not easy, but ITV's Saturday racing coverage was primarily based around a bet. What was most important was showing the race and producing a winner.

My duty on that first day at Ayr, and thereafter on Saturdays until September 1985, was to talk about the runners while they were down at the start, hand over to Raleigh Gilbert or John Penney for the commentary (Graham Goode would normally have been at the principal meeting) and then talk over a slow-motion replay of the closing stages before handing back to Brough, Oaks or Dickie. In terms of a broadcasting role it was not overly demanding. Nor was it overly fulfilling, but I was working on live television and presenting racing – and that was wonderful.

From what I remember Ayr went perfectly fine. What I do remember is that Mark Jackson, one of the richest men in the world, was happy to take us by taxi on the 35-mile journey from Glasgow Airport to Ayr. The fare was £50. I recall thinking that it was a hell of a lot of money to spend. And do you know what? Whenever I now do that same journey more than 30 years later I pay only £35. Isn't that amazing?

There were plenty more chances to make the journey from Glasgow to Ayr in those ITV years and the opportunities given to me by the company were eagerly gobbled up. On those days when ITV covered a midweek meeting I had more chance to be me and to hone the style of presenting I loved most. I was taken away from a desk and allowed to do the roving reporting that ITV had apparently been keen for me to do when I was hired but was just not possible on Saturdays.

I must have been doing something right because the amount of work I was doing for ITV quickly increased. Thames Television, which in those days had the franchise in ITV's London and south east region, asked me if I would like to host a sport programme every Thursday night straight after *News at Ten*. It was a no-brainer. John Bromley, or Bromers to his team, was more than happy for me to take on the programme, and as long as it didn't clash with a midweek ITV racing programme there was never a difficulty in presenting *Thames Sport*. In fact, even if there was ITV racing on a Thursday afternoon – which would not have been that often – I was usually able to get from whichever race-course we were at to the Thames Television studios in plenty of time to prepare for the half-hour programme.

As *Thames Sport* covered what were seen as the main issues at the time, I was able to report on some seriously big stories. Not long after joining ITV I was involved in one of the biggest stories of the time, not so much professionally as personally. It was a story that inspired millions of people and showed my best friend to be not just a fine jockey but a man full of courage. Bob Champion had cancer but he beat it. I watched him do it.

EIGHT

BOB'S FINEST HOUR

EVERYONE knows Bob Champion's story. Everyone knows how he beat cancer, how Aldaniti recovered from a career-threatening injury, and how together horse and rider combined for one of the most famous, popular and emotional victories in the history of the Grand National. You know the story and you might well have seen the film. You know it but I was one of those who lived it. I cried for Bob when I thought he was doomed to die and then rejoiced when, on a memorable afternoon at Aintree, he conquered both cancer and racing's toughest prize.

Unfortunately, I did my rejoicing in front of mum's television. I had been at Aintree for eight consecutive Grand Nationals from 1973 to 1980. I had seen Red Rum win all three of his Nationals and my voice is attached to all three. In 1980 I had been there to commentate on Ben Nevis triumphing under American rider Charlie Fenwick and had I remained with the BBC I would have been at Aintree to see my closest friend and confidant win on Aldaniti. But I did not stay at the BBC and had instead joined ITV only three months earlier. The BBC did the Grand National.

ITV did not. Yet just because BBC1 was broadcasting *Grand National Grandstand*, ITV could not hide away and close down for four hours. The show had to go on and ITV's Saturday afternoon show *World of Sport* did just that. For me that meant an afternoon at Stockton.

In some ways it was good to be at Stockton on Saturday 4 April 1981. The racecourse had long played a special part in my life. It was a local track, full of friends and full of memories that would last forever. There would not, however, be many more memories made at Stockton, or Teesside Park as it was intermittently known in what was always a troubled, precarious life. Various financial crises had been survived but the one that befell it in the early 1980s proved one crisis too many. On Tuesday 16 June 1981, as the racing world fixed its glare on the opening day of Royal Ascot, Stockton staged its final day's racing. Now, where there once was a racecourse, you will find a retail development, fittingly named Teesside Park, in which you'll see a Superdrug, a Morrisons, a Carphone Warehouse and what has been acclaimed as one of the country's most impressive public toilets. Sadly, you will not find any racehorses. They disappeared more than 30 years ago.

So that April Saturday was a chance for me to say some of my goodbyes to Stockton racecourse, but the biggest part of me would have dearly loved to have been at Aintree, even before Aldaniti and Bob completed their heroics. I asked Bromers if he could get me off the shift but it was not possible. For a start I was the obvious presenter for a low-key *World of Sport* card at Stockton. In addition, Brough Scott and Jim McGrath had both been released to do written work at Aintree, as had Oaks, who, ironically for me, was part of BBC Radio's punditry team at the Grand National. There was no way out for me. I would miss my first Grand National in nine years. As the nation watched the BBC at Aintree, I broadcast to hopefully at least a few people from Stockton.

I know I had at least one viewer. Bob. While he was getting ready for the big race he watched *World of Sport*'s Stockton races from the weighing room. The fact that he was physically able to be in the weighing room, or indeed to be anywhere, is astonishing when you consider how ill he had been for much of the preceding two years.

For me, it all started with a phone call. Bob has always loved America and still likes to have his holidays there. I got a call one night from him telling me that he had met a gorgeous vet and was taking her out for dinner that evening. The following day he rang again. I asked how he got on.

'Oh, great,' he said. 'But I've got a problem. She says one of my balls is much harder than it should be. She reckons it might be a problem.'

I tried to put Bob at ease by making a joke.

'I wouldn't worry,' I said. 'The worst that will happen is they'll have you gelded.'

Had I known then what was going to happen, and that Champ would indeed be forced to sacrifice a testicle, I wouldn't have said what I said. Or maybe I would. The two of us have always been incredibly close. He is like a brother to me. I can say anything to him and he can say anything to me. Both of us will know that whatever is said is meant only for the best because we genuinely have the other's interests at heart. We speak every day and I trust him implicitly. There are very, very few people about whom I can say that. I find it exceptionally difficult to trust people outside of my close family but Bob is a glorious exception to the rule. Nobody knows me better and there is nothing I would not do for him.

Whenever my wife Julie kicks me out, I go and stay with Bob. But not long after I had spoken to Bob in America he ended up staying with me in Britain, not in what was then my home in Walton on Thames but in London. I was still working for BBC Radio at the time and had been asked to cover one of showjumping's flagship events, the Horse of the Year Show, at Wembley. The BBC had organised a hotel for me for the duration of the event and I was in my room one evening preparing for the following day when I got a call from Bob asking if he could come and see me.

As soon as he arrived it all came out. Bob had just come from the Royal Marsden Hospital in Sutton. He had bad news, some of the worst news I'd ever heard.

'I've got cancer,' he said.

I told him he was being ridiculous.

'You're 31, you don't drink, you don't smoke, you're a sportsman. Of course you don't have cancer.'

I was wrong. Bob had testicular cancer. He had been given eight months to live unless he received what was then revolutionary new chemotherapy treatment on top of surgery. Had he been diagnosed two years earlier no treatment would have been available to him. He would have died. When we spoke in my room in the London hotel, Bob seemed certain that death was staring him in the face.

Top: My mum and dad, Lillian and Stanley. They are pictured on the day mum became deputy mayor of Teesside. For once, dad was playing the support role. *Bottom:* Tommo the teenager. I'm pictured top left alongside the other members of The Tigers, a band in which I was a drummer. I'm still waiting to get the call to do Glastonbury.

Top: Blondie was the first love of my life. She was virtually unbeatable and I'm riding her here at the Otley Show in Yorkshire, one of many events at which I got to display my showjumping prowess. *Bottom:* Red Rum grabs Crisp at the end of the 1973 Grand National, in which I became the great race's youngest ever commentator when joining the BBC Radio team for the first time at the age of 22 (© Press Association).

Top: Waiting my turn to meet Her Majesty. Bob Champion took me to a Sandringham cocktail party. The Queen sadly turned down my invitation to appear on *The Morning Line*. *Bottom:* My hero. Bob came back from the depths of despair to win the 1981 Grand National on Aldaniti. I could not have a better or braver best friend (© cranhamphoto).

With the future monarch at Plumpton. Prince Charles was smiling and gracious in defeat after our charity race encounter, in which I not only beat him but flashed him as well.

Top left: My second wife, Janie, who did such a wonderful job with our sons Alex (left) and James (right). *Top right:* Peter Bromley, for so long the voice of racing on BBC Radio. He was a truly outstanding commentator (© cranhamphoto). *Bottom:* 'We'll leave that one to the judge!' Tommo in the commentary box, calling the horses (© Phil Smith).

Left: Arriving at the Royal Courts of Justice for my appearance in the Top Cees trial. It was the worst day of my life (© Dan Abraham).
Bottom: The incredible Shergar demolishing the 1981 Derby field. Two years later I found myself involved in unsuccessful attempts to rescue him (© cranhamphoto).

Top: 'That's my son!' James scores a try for Edinburgh in the semi-final of the Heineken Cup in 2012. *Middle:* James and his wife Lyndsey celebrate their Edinburgh wedding in July 2012, alongside Alex, his partner Philippa, mum, my youngest child Hugo, his sister India and a proud father. *Bottom left:* Doesn't Hugo look dapper in his kilt! *Bottom right:* Hey big fellas! When the BBC noticed I was in the crowd watching James playing in the finals of the World Sevens they brought together father and son for an interview.

Top: Some of my happiest memories are from my time in Dubai, all made possible by Sheikh Mohammed, pictured here at Nad Al Sheba alongside Sheikh Hamdan. *Bottom:* Fancy a test drive? Tommo with some of the team behind Newbury's Dubai International Arabian Raceday, the biggest free admission day in racing. If you had come you could have won this little beauty.

Bob spent that night in the room with me but getting sleep was not easy. In the middle of the night it became even harder.

I woke to see Bob stood by the window.

'I'm going to end it all,' he said.

We were on the fifth floor. Had he jumped his chance of surviving would have been slim.

I told him not to be so stupid and to get back into bed. He was genuinely suicidal. He contemplated ending his life but he did not. Instead he spent most of what was left of the night pacing around the room. It was better than what he had been planning before that.

What came next was desperately hard for Bob to endure and desperately hard for those of us who love him to watch. The surgery was gruelling enough but the chemotherapy almost did what the cancer could not quite manage. The treatment nearly killed him. Chemotherapy was brutal back then and at times he could hardly breathe. A man who had ridden hundreds of winners as a jump jockey, a supremely fit individual, was suddenly like a frail old man. I told him he had to keep going and that he needed to stay active. I implored him to keep as busy as possible because he couldn't afford to let his muscles waste. I stressed to him that he was going to need them when he got out of hospital. He listened and he knew I was right but there was one terrible visit when he literally could not get out of bed. As I left the hospital I cried.

'This kid is dying,' I thought to myself. And he was dying, but then he stared death in the face and ordered it to go away.

He recovered, he returned to health, he returned to riding and he made it to Aintree, the place that had been his goal through so much of his punishing treatment. The injury-plagued Aldaniti, who had gone through a considerable ordeal himself just to make it to the Grand National, was waiting for him. The horse's owner Nick Embiricos and trainer Josh Gifford had kept the ride free for Bob. Their loyalty was rewarded.

As soon as my duties at Stockton for *World of Sport* were over I got into the car and sped back to the family home, which was only ten minutes away. There I watched the race with mum. It was a weird experience. Part of me was thinking I should have been at Aintree, as I would have been but for leaving the Beeb, but then all of me started thinking purely about Bob. The race continues to be shown on television every time the Grand National comes around. It is shown because they did it. The runner-up Spartan Missile and his 54-year-old rider John Thorne would have been worthy winners but Aldaniti and Champ were the worthiest possible winners.

I can't imagine what it must feel like to win the Grand National. In the moments that followed Aldaniti's victory I'm not sure that Bob understood, either. People say it takes a while for it all to sink in and I'm sure that applied to Bob. Why else, when he rang me 30 minutes after the race, would the first thing he said to me have been: 'You weren't very good on the telly today.'

I did think that was a slightly strange thing for someone who had just won the National to say.

'I was going to call you earlier,' he said. 'I've had my mind on other things and since the race I've had loads of interviews to do. I mean it, though. You can't afford to keep making mistakes.'

I agreed with Bob that I couldn't afford to keep making mistakes, although all these years later I can't actually remember what mistakes I had made. Bob wasn't being nasty. It was just constructive criticism. He still gives it to me today. He tells me when I've done well. He tells me when I've done not so well. After he had told me what I had done wrong on this particular occasion, he told me what it was like to win the National.

In the years that have followed he has told the story a million times over, including six months later when the reception of his wedding was delayed so that ITV could film an edition of *This Is Your Life* dedicated to Bob. I was Bob's best man but had conspired with the *This Is Your Life* producers to surprise Bob.

'I'll kill you Derek,' were his words at the time. I think he forgave me.

If they ever bring back the big red book there would be plenty to include in a second episode about Bob. In 1983 he founded The Bob Champion Cancer Trust and in 1986 The Bob Champion Cancer Research Unit was opened within the Royal Marsden. Bob has spent much of his time since beating his own cancer trying to help others beat theirs. He has done that through tireless fundraising, which he carries on doing today. When Bob was diagnosed with testicular cancer the survival rate was 35 to 40 per cent. Now, in part thanks to the research work done by Bob's charity, the chance of living is 95 per cent assuming the disease is caught early enough. Today, much of the money that the trust raises is spent on examining the causes and treatment of prostate cancer. If Bob has his way, the survival rate for that potent killer of men will improve as well.

Quite why Bob has never become Sir Bob is hard to fathom, especially when you think of some of the lesser beings who have been awarded knighthoods. Hopefully Bob will one day get that reward. He has been an inspiration to so many people. What seemed like a lifetime after his own epic battle, he was an inspiration to me.

NINE

BEATING THE PRINCE AT PLUMPTON

L ike Lester Piggott, I famously came out of retirement, returned to the saddle and scored a victory that made news around the world. Lester's came aboard Royal Academy in the Breeders' Cup Mile. Mine came aboard Classified in a charity Flat race at Plumpton. Unlike Lester, in my race I beat the heir to the throne.

I had not ridden in a race for more than a decade when I heard about what was being planned at Plumpton. On 4 March, just a few days before the start of the Cheltenham Festival, the diminutive Sussex racecourse was hosting the Mad Hatters Private Sweepstakes, a contest for unlicensed jockeys. I wasn't licensed by anybody so I was eligible. I also quite fancied the challenge. At the time I was living near Hampton Court and so was occasionally making the short drive to Epsom to ride out for some of the local trainers. That meant I hadn't forgotten what to do on a horse and I was also keeping up my general fitness by running quite a bit. (Not a lot of people know this, but I once ran the London Marathon. I didn't win it but I did run it.) I had no doubt that I was physically up for the challenge and I was reluctant to go to my grave with a riding record of no wins, no near-misses and too many falls. There was another attraction to the Mad Hatters race. One of the confirmed riders was the Prince of Wales.

I did not know Prince Charles but I had come into contact with royalty in the past. I had exchanged the odd word with the Queen Mother at her favourite jumps course, Sandown, and spent a very pleasurable hour with her son-in-law, the Duke of Edinburgh. I had been to see him in the late 1970s as part of a BBC Radio preview piece I was doing for the Windsor Horse Show, the event in May that always sits high on the royal family's list of annual highlights. Prince Philip was a noted carriage driver and extremely well respected in the field, which made him an interesting interviewee for the piece, without even taking into account the fact he was married to the Queen. He was an absolute star as well. At the end of the formal recording process he asked me what I was doing for the next hour. I told him I had nothing planned so he said: 'Jump aboard the carriage, then, and we'll go for a drive around Windsor Great Park.'

It was a joy, a real joy. I asked him if it would be okay if I carried on recording our conversation, which he was more than happy for me to do. It made for smashing radio with the piece ending up being featured on the prestigious *Pick of the Week* highlights programme. He was driving four horses and made it look easy, even though it clearly was not. Now and again he got a bit agitated with the horses, and he did use a few words that I'm sure he never lets out in front of Her Majesty, but even after all the bleeps were taken out we still had plenty of material.

Unlike the Queen, Prince Philip has never really seemed to take too much interest in racing and it's often said that as soon as the royal procession is completed at Royal Ascot he gets in a car and goes straight back to Windsor Castle. Slightly more interested than his father is Prince Charles, who in 1980 had decided that he would quite like to ride in a race. Plumpton provided the perfect opportunity and his participation no doubt helped the charities involved raise a considerable sum. To take part you had to stump up £200, which in those days was a somewhat chunkier sum than it is today. On BBC wages I couldn't afford to pay that much myself, so I set about trying to find a sponsor. The answer to my prayers came in the form of Bob Dean, the business partner of one of my BBC colleagues, television showjumping commentator Raymond Brooks-Ward, who sadly died all too young at the age of 62. Bob was one of the three founders of the famous cinema advertising company Pearl & Dean (the one with the catchy jingle). When I mentioned the race to Bob at one of the major horse shows he said there and then that he would sponsor and handed me the £200. All I needed now was a horse.

For that I shall be eternally grateful to Nicky Henderson. In the 2012-2013 jumps season Nicky regained the trainers' championship and was responsible for one of the all-time great chasers in Sprinter Sacre, but in my eyes his greatest achievement will always be in having sent out Classified to win the Mad Hatters race. To have found a horse that even I could win on was some feat, although perhaps it was my association with Classified that turned him from a horse that nobody at Seven Barrows seemed to know about into a high-class jumper who subsequently finished fifth and then third in the Grand National.

I happened to know the owner of Classified, who had bought the horse at Newmarket but was not holding out a great deal of hope for his new purchase. On the basis that he had no great plans for the seemingly moderate animal, Nicky, in those days still a young man, was asked to prepare him for Plumpton. Keen to make a decent fist of my comeback, I made regular trips up the M4 to Lambourn and began riding out twice a week for Nicky, getting to know Classified at the same time. The horse was clearly no superstar, and he had the tendency to be a bit bad-tempered, but he felt better and better the more I rode him. Then on the Sunday before the race he showed just how much better he had become.

Nicky often works some of his best horses on the Sunday before the Festival. Classified was not one of his best inmates – or at least not at the time – but with the Plumpton race taking place just two days later, Nicky wanted to give the horse a final blowout before the big day. (It probably wasn't a big day to Nicky but it was to Tommo!) Nicky had been an excellent amateur rider so he took part in the three-horse gallop, as did his stable jockey Steve Smith Eccles. It was an incredible exercise because Classified won it by what must have been at least 25 lengths.

As we pulled up I looked around and said to myself: 'Oh crap. I must have gone too fast.' I was preparing myself for what would have been the biggest rollicking of my life only to discover I wasn't going to get one.

'What the hell were you doing there?' asked Steve.

'I'm sorry Ecc. I must have got a bit carried away,' I said.

'Don't apologise son,' he said, a big smile on his face. 'That horse I was riding won a handicap hurdle at Newbury carrying top weight last time. You've just given me two stones and annihilated him. Bloody hell! You are now sitting on what will be the biggest certainty ever to come out of Nicky Henderson's yard.'

'Oh, that's nice,' I thought. I had started my Plumpton plan thinking that it would be lovely to win a race for the first time, but until that mind-blowing Sunday gallop I didn't really have much expectation of the dream coming true. Now I did.

I was clearly on a good horse but so was Prince Charles. He was riding Long Wharf, a very useful youngster who was being prepared by one of the Queen's trainers, Ian Balding. The bookmakers had made him favourite but there was plenty of money from within Seven Barrows for Classified. As I got to Plumpton, Bob Champion, who was also there that day, told me that Corky Browne, Nicky's head lad then and now, had backed Classified.

'Corky wanted to let you know that his own money is down,' said Bob. 'It means you've got a pretty good chance of winning. It also means that if you get beat Corky and the other lads in the yard will probably put out a contract on you.'

That was pressure. Added pressure came from the fact I was wearing a set of breeches that had been loaned to me by the trainer. Nicky would be the first to admit that he comes from quite a well-heeled background and has never been short of a few quid, but you wouldn't have known it from the state of his breeches. They looked like a family heirloom from the previous century. They had clearly fallen apart more than once and it was only through a large amount of stitched repair jobs that they were still in one piece – and only just in one piece. Unfortunately for me, they began to come apart at the seams as I cantered Classified down to Plumpton's two-mile start. As we circled around waiting to be called in for the race the studs popped open. I was still playing with my flies trying to rectify the situation when the starter called us into line. This was hardly ideal.

The breeches problem aside, I had a pretty clear head and knew what I wanted to do. Although I hadn't ridden in a race for many years, I did at least have some race-riding experience, something most of the others in the contest lacked. Prince Charles was making his debut as a jockey and he was not alone in being a racing virgin. I reckoned I had to use a bit of the knowledge I'd amassed. I knew Plumpton well and was certain the best place to be on a tight track that turns quite a bit was the inside. Stay close to the rail and you saved ground by going the shortest way round. My intention was to sit in second place before firing Classified into the lead taking the home bend. And that's what happened.

In the early stages a girl was carted past me by her horse and went into the lead. She was all over the place so I decided to let her go. Classified was travelling like a dream. As we galloped past the railway station on the second circuit with less than half a mile to go I was feeling confident.

'Come on big fella,' I said. 'Let's move up a gear.'

I asked the question and he answered it. We moved into the lead but I still hadn't gone for everything. I was keen to save our maximum effort until we came off that final bend, which I wanted to use as a slingshot. At exactly the spot I'd intended I slapped my horse down the neck. Never before have I felt such power emanating from between my legs. He went whoosh! It was the greatest feeling in the world. Never once in all those races I rode in at the Cattericks, Sedgefields and Newcastles of this world had I felt anything like this before. All the way up the home straight I had a smile on my face. In fact, I think I even broke into a chuckle. Was I loving it? Yes I was.

But it wasn't down to me, it was down to the horse. He was a machine that day at Plumpton, completely free of fault. Sadly, and most embarrassingly for me, the same was not true of Nicky Henderson's breeches. They gave me trouble at the start and they gave me trouble at the finish because they split open on the run-in, at precisely the point where the Prince of Wales, our future king no less, had moved into second and also into a position where he had an eyefull of my backside. To journalists it was a dream come true and my ignominy prompted one newspaper to print a picture of the finish under the headline: 'The Outsider who flashed past the Prince!'

I had revealed a little more of myself than I had wanted, but I had won! HRH finished two lengths behind me in second, and although disappointed with himself for not winning, he was the most gracious of losers. He was also a very fit loser. Back in the weighing room I couldn't believe how little he was blowing. He said that with a bit more experience he might have finished closer but he was in no way complaining and he said he had really enjoyed himself. Given how well he was talking I thought it would be great to get him back into the winner's enclosure for an interview. Very kindly he agreed and so I got hold of a microphone and interviewed him for the public. Imagine that. To be beaten by me and interviewed by me in the space of ten minutes! I might even have said that to him! I asked him some funny questions, which I could tell he appreciated. It's just possible that I addressed him as 'big fella' as well.

Another nice aspect of the race was that Brough Scott did the one and only live commentary of his broadcasting career. Brough, who has always mixed well with royalty and is probably a bit royal himself, was a perfect choice, but he did tell me after the race that he wouldn't do it again. He once had a trial run at doing it for ITV – although not on air – but he found the binoculars too heavy to lift through the race so he had to stop. And that's a true story!

Brough might not have commentated again but Prince Charles did ride again. I'm afraid to say, though, that our next king will not be able to say he ever rode a winner. He had five more rides but, just like me all those years earlier, he developed an unfortunate habit of falling off. He did finish second once at Ludlow on a horse called Allibat but he was also unseated twice within the space of five days from his own horse, Good Prospect, firstly at Sandown and then on the biggest stage of all at the Cheltenham Festival. That sparked a few murmurings from people who felt it wasn't right for a future monarch to be risking his neck riding over fences, especially as he was due to get married a few weeks later.

So the Queen never got to see her son ride a winner. I'm pleased to say that my parents did, although neither mum nor dad were there in the flesh at Plumpton. Nevertheless, there is a lovely story concerning dad, which says a lot about what he was like. While the Plumpton race was being run he took out one of his horses and walked it to a big field owned by one of his friends, a farmer called Mr Buckle. Dad wanted to be riding at a gallop at the same time his boy was riding in a race against royalty. At precisely the time my race was being run dad was on horseback himself. He brought the horse back to a halt as he got to the farmer's house, where Mr Buckle was standing outside the front door waiting for dad.

'Stan,' he said. 'Derek's won the race. He's won! He's done it.'

It was a 20-minute walk back to his house but I reckon dad walked that walk as the proudest man in Britain. He did everything he possibly could for me. This was one thing I was able to give back to him. He has now been gone for 30 years and I still miss him. When he died I cradled him in my arms and cried my eyes out. I owed him everything then and still do to this day. The day I beat Prince Charles at Plumpton was for Stanley Thompson.

Prince Charles doesn't get to Newmarket very often, and even less frequently to Redcar, so our paths have not crossed that often since Plumpton, but there was one particularly memorable meeting of the former Mad Hatters.

It took place during Royal Ascot at York in 2005. I was working there for At The Races but was not on duty at the time. The prince was on the podium presenting a trophy along with Camilla, who I noticed making eye contact with me. After the prizes had been handed over she started walking towards me.

'Blimey,' I thought to myself. 'I'm going to have an audience.' And I did.

'I know you,' Camilla said to me. 'You're the one who beat my future husband.'

Then Prince Charles joined us and we exchanged some pleasantries. We had a lovely conversation, during which he asked me if I fancied a rematch?

'Sir,' I said. 'I'd love to, but you're far too old!'

We all laughed at that one.

Then it got even better. Sheikh Mohammed spotted us and walked across to say hello.

'Derek, how are you?' he asked me, after which I said: 'Sir, have you met Prince Charles and Camilla?'

To be fair, he probably had, but that didn't occur to me at the time.

I couldn't believe it. Me, the kid from Middlesbrough, was chatting away with three royals at once. And for some reason, they were the ones who wanted to talk to me! I'm not ashamed to say I had to go and ring my mother to pass on the news.

I wouldn't have told my wife because Julie isn't a royalist. She wouldn't get rid of them but she also doesn't see the need to bow down to them, either. For that reason she didn't come along when I was invited to a cocktail party at Sandringham. There were about 40 of us at the event, all waiting for the chance to talk to the Queen. I was there with Bob Champion, who she knows very well, so she had quite a long conversation with Bob before moving across to me.

It slightly embarrasses me to have to admit it, but I said something to her I probably should not have said. Me being me, I couldn't resist.

'Ma'am,' I said. 'Would you please come on *The Morning Line*?'

She paused for a second, clearly weighing up the possible pros and cons of the offer.

'Does that mean I would have to meet Mr McCririck,' she inquired.

'Yes Ma'am, I'm afraid you unfortunately would,' I answered.

'Well therefore Mr Thompson,' she said, 'I might have to decline your invitation.'

We never did get her on the programme. I'm sure she was a regular viewer, though.

TEN

DERBY DAYS, 007 AND A RUDE ROD STEWART

During my time at ITV, and for the first decade of the Channel 4 era that followed, Derby Day was our big day. It was our crown jewel and by far the most prestigious event we covered. In 1995, Channel 4 took over the Cheltenham Festival, which became our principal priority, but in 1981, when I took part in my maiden television Derby, Epsom on the first Wednesday in June was everything. It was also one of the rare occasions when the whole of the ITV team came together – and when we came together for the Derby in 1981, we did so for something very special.

Shergar's Derby was not, of course, the first Derby in which I had been involved. I had worked on the previous eight runnings of the race for BBC Radio, generally as a reporter and supporting member of the squad, but most memorably for me in 1979 when I presented coverage of the 200th Derby. The honour was not meant to have fallen to me, and it would not have done had Des Lynam not been struck down by illness. Des had been due to anchor not only the Derby but also an England football match in a major sporting double-header on Radio 2. On the morning of the race I got a phone call from the office to tell me Des was poorly and I would have to stand in for him at Epsom in the racing part of the programme. It remains one of the highlights of my career, not only because Troy was such a wonderful winner, and his rider Willie Carson was so entertaining in the post-race interviews, but because the job I did that afternoon was so well received.

Anyone who knows me will testify that I hate to blow my own trumpet, but I do think I proved an able deputy for the big man. I was particularly proud of the way I ended the broadcast, which I did with a sign-off that went like this:

> 'The crowds are leaving Epsom, some richer, some poorer, some a little worse for wear. But they will remember this day for a very long time because they were here for the 200th Derby and they saw a horse who could have been one of the greatest Derby winners of all time. From all of us at Epsom, good night.'

For me, it was a very good night. I had loved the chance to take the top billing for a change and I felt I had done the role justice. Others seemed to think so, too, including the long-serving *Test Match Special* commentator Don Mosey, who wrote me a lovely letter, in which he said that my performance at Epsom had been perfect and that I was 'the most gifted broadcaster working on radio'. It was all very flattering but I never got a job on *Test Match Special*, which is a pity as I love cake.

I also love the Derby and have done since I was a young boy. I well remember nipping out of lessons at Guisborough Grammar

School to listen to the commentary on the wireless. One of my favourite winners was Sir Ivor, who finished so strongly to win under Lester Piggott. I remember that race particularly fondly because a film was made, entitled *The Year of Sir Ivor*, that I watched at a screening organised by the Racegoers Club, which I had just joined.

By the time Shergar entered the stalls for the 1981 Derby I had also just joined the ITV team. On most Saturdays we were a divided team, not in terms of friendships or morale, but physically, as some of us would have been at one meeting, and the rest at another meeting. There were very few occasions when we all worked together in the same place, but Derby Day was one such occasion. We all stayed together in a hotel not far from the course, and on the night before Shergar's Derby about 50 of us had enjoyed a little party in my room that went on until 1am. We were young enough to get away with it in those days and *The Morning Line* hadn't been invented, either! These days I need to be in bed by 9pm.

Even after a party I woke up on the morning of Shergar's Derby feeling bright, breezy and tremendously excited. We had covered Shergar running away with what was then known as the Guardian Classic Trial at Sandown and the BBC had televised him romping to victory in the Chester Vase. Not surprisingly he was sent off a red-hot favourite, although with hindsight it's astonishing he was as big as 10-11 when the race began. I'm sure that had the race been run today he would have been a much shorter favourite. Everyone knows that he won the race more like a 1-10 favourite with Peter Bromley famously saying in his radio commentary that, 'you'll need a telescope to see the rest'. Also famous is the story about John Matthias, rider of the runner-up Glint Of Gold, having ended the race believing he had won because Shergar was so far clear in the distance that he could not see him. Apparently he only realised the truth when he was pulling up Glint Of Gold and saw Walter Swinburn on Shergar heading to that iconic winner's circle in the opposite direction!

I was the first one to get to Walter, who was barely out of short trousers at the time, but had already achieved the thing that would live with him for longer than anything. Walter as a rider was never the chattiest in interviews, but even that day, with so little experience on the biggest stage behind him, he was still better than Shergar's trainer Michael Stoute. Walter's then boss, whom we know now as Sir Michael, is famously lacking in words when it comes to interviews with reporters and journalists, surprisingly so for a man who first came to Britain hoping to get the BBC job that was taken by Julian Wilson. Sir Michael is often very difficult to get anything out of, but in 1981, when a much younger man, he was just as bad. Almost all my questions were returned with answers that consisted of two, three or, if I was lucky, maybe four words. Nothing has changed. I find that a great shame.

It was easier to forgive Lester Piggott his reticence following Teenoso's victory in 1983. Lester was never destined to be an after-dinner speaker on retirement but he also had the excuse of being deaf in one ear when displaying his occasionally abrupt nature. Even so, I was a bit taken aback with the way he greeted me when I pushed a microphone in his direction as he walked Teenoso back up the racecourse.

'F**k off,' was how he started and stopped his half of a conversation that was broadcast live. Fortunately, Lester's sometimes muffled voice could be hard to decipher at the best of times and, thankfully, this was one of the not-so-good times. It also has to be pointed out that he was not so much angry with me but with the swarm of photographers, notably David Hastings, who in his opinion were getting in the way of his horse. Tact and diplomacy were never among Lester's strong points.

Over the years I got some better interviews with Lester, but even if he didn't always play ball at Epsom, plenty of others did. For those of us on ITV, and then on Channel 4, the Derby was seen as our chance to get a few famous faces on the screen. In the 1980s there seemed to be a conscious effort on the part of Epsom and the Derby's organisers to bring in the celebrities. It was felt they added glamour to the afternoon, but my own opinion was that it was the horses and the racing that interested most people. Understandably, though, if there were stars of stage and screen present, we had to get them on the programme.

None seemed to get on the programme as much as Joan Collins. I've nothing against old Joan, and I wouldn't argue with those who say that Alexis Colby remains one of the greatest television soap bitches of all time. I even loved those TV adverts she did with Leonard Rossiter. It has to be said, though, that interviewing Joan could get a bit on the dull side. I also think it has to be said that interviewing celebrities in general can be dull. I became associated with being the one who took on the task of doing the celebrity interviews, but, personally, I always believed they detracted from the show. We had to do it because housewives were watching and it was felt they would enjoy a sprinkling of stardust on the programme, but so many of the celebs were boring and irritating. The most illuminating thing they tended to tell you is that they had just backed the last winner. So what? I probably tipped it on my hotline.

Now and again you do find one who makes it worthwhile, someone like Tommy Steele or Bing Crosby, who I spoke to once and found utterly fascinating. He was an old man but he came alive when he realised he had an audience. Also fantastic was Larry Hagman, JR Ewing from *Dallas*, who I interviewed during Channel 4's first Prix de l'Arc de Triomphe in 1986. When Larry saw me waving to him in the paddock he very kindly came over, accompanied by his Southfork wife, Linda 'Sue Ellen' Gray. I almost couldn't believe it was happening. *Dallas* was huge in those days and JR was just about the most famous character on television. I called him JR – I knew he'd like that! – and then asked him whether, as a rich oil baron from Texas, he owned any racehorses? He came back with a great answer: 'No sir,' he said. 'I don't like anything that eats while I sleep!'

I loved that.

Sue Ellen, or Linda as I grew to know her, was marvellous as well. Years later, in 2007 to be precise, I got a phone call from the actor John Bowe, who said that he and Linda were coming to Cambridge and Linda wondered if she would be able to see the horses exercising in Newmarket.

'You bet,' I said. I can't tell you how excited I was picking up Linda in my Mercedes and seeing her sitting in the passenger seat. Wow! What a lovely lady. She and John were appearing together in a play called Terms Of Endearment at the time and Linda made sure that my wife Julie and I were given free tickets to see her. Both Mr and Mrs Thompson had a superb night and it got even better afterwards as Linda invited us into her dressing room. I know Julie won't mind me saying this, but she and Linda, who was 67 at the time, looked like sisters. Linda is such a beautiful woman, absolutely stunning, and she has one of the best heads of hair I've ever seen.

Other soap stars have become dear friends, people like the *Coronation Street* actors Charlie Lawson and Mikey North, both of whom love their racing, and I could not write this book without mentioning one of my very best mates, Frazer Hines, for so many years a heartthrob in both *Doctor Who* and *Emmerdale*. I'm also still a good friend of Frazer's ex-wife Liz Hobbs, the most famous female British water-skier in the history of the sport. She once rang me up and asked if I could pass on a telephone number for Epsom racecourse as she wanted to put on a pop concert after one of the track's evening meetings. I gave her the number and now Liz's music nights have changed the face of evening racing in Britain. Thanks to her, the likes of Madness, Meat Loaf, the Kaiser Chiefs, Happy Mondays and Ronan Keating appeared on British racecourses over the space of just a couple of months in the summer of 2013.

Some of the other best celebrity interviews I've done were conducted at Sandown on Variety Club day. I must have presented Channel 4's coverage from that meeting 25 times. I loved it. Sometimes we didn't always get the very biggest names, which was a shame, but I got to have a real laugh with the comedians. One of my funniest moments at Sandown came with Bert Kwouk, who was most famous for playing Inspector Clouseau's man-servant Cato in the *Pink Panther* films. I met him before we went on air and arranged for him to come up behind me and try to karate chop me while I was talking to the camera. As he did it,

I turned to him and said: 'Not now, Cato, you stupid fool.' Oh, I loved that as well. If you haven't seen a *Pink Panther* film none of what I've just said will mean anything to you, but if you have seen the films I'm sure you would have chuckled. I'm chuckling now just thinking about it.

But nobody made me chuckle as much as Eric Morecambe. My second ever *World of Sport* broadcast was from Warwick and Eric was there with his little Ern raising money for charity. I rang up the boss Andrew Franklin and asked him if I could get them on the programme, which wasn't easy as there was never much spare time during an ITV6 or ITV7. Andrew knew you couldn't turn down an opportunity like that so I asked the boys if they would mind appearing on the programme. In the end only Eric came on but he was superb, mucking about with me and doing that funny thing he used to do with his glasses and a white handkerchief.

Sadly, not everybody was as nice as Bert and Eric. Sir Bruce Forsyth has always been one of my heroes but I found him very poor as an interviewee, not once but twice. Both times I've interviewed him we've had to do it on the run. Over the years I've amassed almost as many catchphrases as Bruce, so if he had played ball we could have done something great together, but he didn't want to join in the fun. I once interviewed him for At The Races at Royal Ascot and he made clear he was doing it under sufferance. That's a shame. I know some people think he is dated, but I still find him very funny and I once had a wonderful night with dad watching Bruce perform in a theatre. They say you should never meet your heroes, and for me that proved to be the case with Bruce. Funnily enough, I've asked lots of taxi drivers which of their famous passengers they have found most disappointing. So many of them have said Bruce. I might have ruined my chance of ever being invited to do *Strictly Come Dancing* but sometimes you've just got to speak what you believe is the truth.

I'm afraid I also had an unpleasant experience with James Bond. I was at Murrayfield in February 2012 for the Six Nations Calcutta Cup match between Scotland and England. I was sat not far from the royal box and noticed that just behind me was the latest James Bond, the actor Daniel Craig, who it turns out is quite short when he's not playing 007. He was wearing a big woolly hat, presumably in an attempt to disguise himself, but he was sat within feet of me so I thought there was no harm in trying to say hello. I wanted to introduce myself and bring up in conversation his Bond colleague Dame Judi Dench, who has racehorses in training with Mark Tompkins in Newmarket. I never got the chance. As I turned around and began to open my mouth, the bloke sat next to him said bluntly: 'Please don't interrupt Mr Craig. He's here to watch the rugby.' I explained that I was just hoping to have a quick word but instead the minder gave me a few quick words back in return. They were not very nice and nor was Mr Craig, who did not even allow himself to make eye contact with me.

I'm pleased to say there was a pleasant sequel to what happened. Sat in the royal box was Scotland's first minister, Alex Salmond. My political views are very different to those of Alex, but whilst I often don't agree with him I have always found him to be a smashing man and I admire him greatly. He is a massive racing fan and made a point of making himself available to come on *The Morning Line* once a year while I was the presenter. That was extremely good of him as he works incredibly hard, so hard in fact that I once saw him looking completely wiped out. I was worried for him and asked him why he put himself through it? 'Because I love it Tommo,' was his simple answer. That made me like him even more, as did his actions that afternoon at Murrayfield. From his luxurious position in the royal box Alex saw me in the stands. 'Tommo, Tommo,' he shouted. 'How are you doing? Come and join us in here.' I thought that was so kind of him. I spent the rest of the afternoon with Alex in the royal box while Daniel Craig was left sat out in the cold. It might only have been a little victory but it meant a lot.

And while I'm on a roll I've got to say that I once had an unpleasant experience with another diminutive international star, Rod Stewart. I was working for the radio station talkSPORT at Windsor one Monday night when I happened to see Rod. I went over to him, perfectly politely as always, and asked him if Tommo could have an interview. All he said back to me was: 'F**k off!'

There and then I vowed never again to buy one of his records. And do you know what? I've been true to my word. Having said that, I do rather like Rod's wife Penny Lancaster. She is outstanding. I once interviewed her and I found her to be very agreeable. I also found her to be extremely tall and statuesque, which must make life difficult for such a short husband.

As lovely as Penny was, and I'm sure still is, I do find that most celebrities are a bit boring. On Derby Day, and all racing days, it's the horses that interest me the most. And few horses have interested me as much as Shergar. Working on his Derby win was a joy. When he came back into my life two years later it was much less of a pleasure.

ELEVEN

TRYING TO SAVE SHERGAR

As I write this, 30 years have passed since I took on perhaps the unlikeliest role of my career. I have been asked to do some strange things in my time, and more often than not I've said yes, but not even I ever expected to become a kidnap negotiator. The story has been told so many times over the intervening three decades. To my great sadness, the story's end always remains the same with Shergar never found, either dead or alive.

It was in the early hours of Wednesday 9 February 1983, that Shergar came back into my life. He had last been in it when I was part of a television Derby for the first time in June 1981. I had been working for ITV that afternoon at Epsom when perhaps the greatest of all Derby winners carried Walter Swinburn to an almost unbelievably easy victory in the most famous and cherished of all Flat races. He had raced for the final time when sensationally beaten in the St Leger but that was quite plainly not the real Shergar. Tragically, the real Shergar was the one who at just after 8.30pm on the night of Tuesday 8 February 1983, was kidnapped from the Aga Khan's Ballymanny Stud in County

105

Kildare by three armed men. Jim Fitzgerald, Shergar's groom, was told that £2 million was needed for his safe return.

My involvement started at 1.45am on the Wednesday morning. I was staying in a London hotel because the following evening I was due to present *Thames Sport*. When the phone went my first reaction was that it must be the hotel's reception ringing me with my 7.30am alarm call. But it wasn't. On the other end of the phone was a reporter from the Press Association who had rung to tell me that I was one of three British journalists that the supposed kidnappers of Shergar had demanded go to Belfast and help in the recovery of the superstar horse. In my bleary state, what was being said made precious little sense. All these years later it still beggars belief.

The phone rang again at 7am. This time it was Bob Champion, ringing to tell me the news that the phone call in the middle of the night had already become public knowledge. Almost as soon as I put down the phone to Bob it was ringing again with a journalist wanting to know what I was going to do. After I had spoken to that journalist there was another journalist and then another after him. Suddenly I was hot property. I tried to clear my mind with a jog before breakfast but there was too much going on in my head for there to be any hope of gaining a sense of clarity. Breakfast failed to help, so I went into the *Thames Sport* office and asked what I should do. I had a live programme to present, so dashing off to Belfast was hardly practical, but at the same time I could never have forgiven myself if I had not gone to Belfast and something had happened to the horse as a direct result. I had already been in touch with one of the other two journalists that had been ordered to Belfast, my ITV colleague John Oaksey. He had arranged to get an early afternoon flight to Belfast. I did not really know the other journalist, *The Sun*'s Peter Campling, but I soon would.

Without trying to be self-deprecating, we were an unusual trio to pick. I read subsequently someone suggesting that whoever picked us must have been a reader of *The Sun* who was watching the ITV Seven the previous Saturday as John had been presenting from Sandown, I had been on duty at Stratford and Peter was an ITV Seven tipster for *The Sun*. Aside from that, there was nothing that linked the three of us, but however tenuous the connection, we were there together, boarding a plane to Northern Ireland at Heathrow Airport, surrounded by a gaggle of TV, radio and newspaper reporters. It was, to say the least, surreal.

At Belfast we were met by a car that had been organised by the ITV news provider ITN. It ferried us to our appointed point of rendezvous, the Europa Forum Hotel. On the way there, the driver, a man called Sebastian Rich, who as an ITN cameraman had filmed in some of the world's most dangerous places, kept pointing out the places of interest, as if we were on a sightseeing tour of the city. We most definitely were not and some of the sights Seb showed us I certainly did not want to see. It turned into a guided tour of the Troubles. At one point he took a turn off into an area that looked exceptionally unfriendly.

'I don't like the look of this place,' I remember saying to Seb, who got us to the Europa with at least one of his passengers by now feeling more than a bit anxious. What happened next hardly helped my nerves.

Just after I had checked in to the most regularly bombed hotel in Belfast (a nice touch, that) an announcement went out asking for a Mr Derek Thompson to go to the foyer, where there was a telephone call waiting for him. Something inside me told me that this wasn't going to be good.

I picked up the phone and listened.

'Mr Derek Thompson?'

All he said was my name but it was obvious that he was checking it was me. I agreed that it was.

'You're the one who does the ITV?' he asked again in a pretty unremarkable Irish accent.

'What did you do before that?'

It was as if he was trying to hire me for a job and wanted to confirm my working history.

'Well, I was on Radio 2 for about nine years doing the sport on there,' I said.

'Oh, oh.' he said. Nothing more, just 'oh, oh'.

By now it seemed fair enough to ask to whom I was having the pleasure of talking.

'My name's Arkle,' he said.

'As in the horse?' I asked.

'Yes,' he said, before adding with menace in his voice: 'We've got Shergar.'

He clearly wasn't trying to book me for a job.

'Now listen,' he said. 'This is what I want you to do. Get in contact with Mrs Jeremy Maxwell. Give them a ring at this particular number and you'll then be given further instructions as to what to do.'

The line went dead. I put the phone down, turned around and saw a fair percentage of Britain and Ireland's journalists looking straight at me.

'Well that's very interesting,' I said, after which I was bombarded with questions. 'Could you just give me a chance to get my thoughts?' I said, telling them I was going to go up to my room. That's exactly what I did.

Once in the room I phoned the number I had been given and found myself speaking to someone who called himself 'a law man' and told me how to get to the farm of the Maxwells, a race-horse training family. He also gave me the number of the local police station, which I rang and got confirmation that the man I had been speaking to was indeed a police officer. For obvious reasons, it seemed best to double check everything. The news reassured me but the policeman in the station also asked me if I could do my best to make sure I wasn't followed to the farm by the press. That was always going to be easier said than done. I did a piece to camera for *Thames Sport* – there is no point being on the trail of the hottest story in town and not making something of it – and then called Oaks and Peter to my room, as well as the hotel's chief of security. I asked him how we could get out of the hotel without the journalists spotting us. He showed us a way, that duly took us through the kitchens, out of the back door, into the car and then off into Belfast, sometimes travelling at 90 miles per hour.

We sped off to Downpatrick, home of one of Northern Ireland's two racecourses and also home to the Maxwells. I sensed we were being followed by at least one press car – which happened to include ITN's Jeremy Thompson, now one of the leading presenters for Sky News – but soon enough that was not my biggest concern. As we approached our destination five guys jumped out into the road. Every one of them was wearing a balaclava and holding a machine gun. I said a swear word under my breath. I thought they were going to spray us with gunfire and kill us on the spot. What I had forgotten was that the officer in the police station had told us we would be met by some of his colleagues. I suppose I had thought they would be wearing the uniforms they wore while on the beat. It turned out I was wrong.

One of the five men came to the passenger window where I was sitting. Quite why I seemed to be the one being picked for everything I don't know. I just wish I hadn't been. He gestured at me to wind down my window, so, gulping while I did it, I did as I had been told. We came face to face, or at least we would have done had I been able to see his face. All I actually could see was a mouth and two eyes that were looking through holes cut out of the balaclava.

'Are you Derek Thompson?' he asked me.

I was put on the spot. What would you have said in the circumstances? I could have said, 'No, I'm Brough Scott' and hoped they believed me. I know Brough had been a little put out that he wasn't one of the three journalists sent over to Belfast so by saying I was him – and a lot of people often confuse the two of us, which I think pleases Brough – I would at least have got him involved. But I didn't say that. I told the truth.

'Yes, I'm Derek Thompson,' I said, hoping to goodness that had been the right thing to do. Thankfully, it was.

He told me they were all with the police and directed me towards the house, where we met the trainer Jeremy Maxwell, his wife Judy and poor old Richard Pitman, who had gone over to Northern Ireland trying to buy horses but had managed to get himself caught up in a major terrorist incident. Even at that stage everyone assumed that a terrorist incident was what this was. Nobody really believed that Shergar had not been taken by the IRA. Someone had mooted that maybe Colonel Gaddafi was involved but the consensus was that this was very much an IRA crime.

When we got to the house we learnt that 'Arkle' had already rung once but Jeremy had been on the toilet, so Judy had taken the call. She had been told that 'Arkle' was changing his name to that of another well-known horse, 'Ekbalco', and that the ransom demand had also been altered, from the initial £2m to just £40,000. That seemed very odd indeed but made some sense in that there were 40 shares in Shergar, six of them retained by the Aga Khan, the other 34 all sold to individual shareholders. Right from the start that meant the kidnappers did not merely have to persuade the Aga that paying a ransom was the right thing to do. They had to get the approval of 35 people, a factor they surely had not realised when the plan was hatched. They were not only evil men. They had also failed to do their research.

All of us then sat waiting and looking at the telephone, which the police had tapped so that any conversations could be recorded, provided that they were of a length that made taping possible. At around 8.30pm the phone stirred into action. It was 'Ekbalco'. He repeated his demand for £40,000 and ordered us to get that message put out on the BBC evening news bulletin. None of us could decide if we were dealing with one of the kidnappers or a hoaxer. Oaks seemed to think this was all rubbish and that I had been speaking to either a nutter or someone trying to make an easy £40,000. My opinion was that I was speaking to a member of the IRA but it made no difference which of us was right. We had to continue dealing with 'Ekbalco' in the hope that he was genuine.

I had an idea. I thought it would be useful to speak to the Aga Khan. Unfortunately I didn't have his number. Instead I rang Shergar's former trainer, Michael Stoute, who gave me the number for the Ballymany stud manager Ghislain Drion, who in turn passed me on to the man he said the Aga had dispatched to represent him, a well-spoken Englishman called David Watson. When I spoke to him, Mr Watson was bordering on useless and seemed to have no interest in what I was saying. He seemed convinced that we were dealing with a hoaxer and spoke to me more as though I was a journalist trying to bother him for a story, as opposed to someone who had flown to Northern Ireland in an effort to save his employer's horse. I was more than a bit annoyed.

At about 10.30pm we received another call, this time from a lady who said she was putting us through to the Aga Khan, who spoke to Jeremy and asked how much money the kidnappers now wanted. Jeremy told him. He said he would ring back, which he did.

'Proceed, we'll pay,' he said.

We rang the BBC immediately and got them to report this breaking news in the final BBC1 evening bulletin, which was going out before closedown and the test card at 11.45pm. That, regrettably, had been the wrong thing to do. After the news announcer had told the world that the Aga Khan was prepared to pay the £40,000 ransom, we began to repeatedly play back what the Aga Khan had said. When you listened hard you could hear that His Highness was speaking with an Irish accent and was finishing off his sentences with the words, 'you know'. We had been duped but whoever duped us was a pretty good actor because initially he had us well and truly fooled.

It was frustrating but there was more frustration to come. After midnight the man who had been 'Arkle' before becoming 'Ekbalco' rang again, although by now he was using yet another codename. He wanted £1,000 for 'a picture of the pony' and said that he would regard that as 'a goodwill gesture'. At 1.30am he rang back.

'Derek,' he said. 'I'm beginning to think that you think I'm a hoax.'

'No, we don't think you're a hoax,' I said. 'Put yourself in my position. Now what would you think if a guy kept ringing up all the time?'

'Well I'm not a hoax,' he said. 'We have got Shergar, and if you don't give us the money by nine o'clock in the morning we'll shoot him.'

Unbeknownst to the caller, I had been a bit crafty. As an interviewer you need to know how to get the best out of an interviewee. You need to keep the interviewee talking and that's what I had done, so much so that he had been on the phone for more than a minute and a half, which was enough for the police to have traced the call. I asked one of the officers if they could now work out from where the caller had been ringing.

'Mr Thompson,' he said. 'I'm sorry to say the officer who traces calls went off shift at midnight.'

I was flabbergasted. History tells us that the police handling of the whole Shergar case was pitifully bad. This was just one example of that. Here was a huge crime that was being investigated by the equivalent of the Keystone Cops, whose team was headed by a chief superintendent called Jim 'Spud' Murphy, who employed clairvoyants, psychics and diviners to help the search and who once famously said: 'A clue, that is what we haven't got.' And he didn't have a clue. Not one.

Just after 7am on what was now Thursday morning, by which point John and Peter had gone back to the hotel, my man rang again. Judy took the call.

'Hello, this is Arkle,' he said, reverting to the original code-name. 'The horse has had an accident and we've put him down.'

Judy asked where the horse's body could be found.

'He's dead,' said Arkle bluntly and put the phone down. And that was that.

The claim that Shergar had been destroyed convinced the police that this had all been a hoax. What we had not known was that all the time we had been dealing with my phone caller, the Dublin police had been carrying out their own investigation, one that was quite separate to that being undertaken by the Kildare division. Both, it seemed, were equally hapless.

Back in the hotel I read an exclusive piece in the *Daily Star* written by Derek Thompson, in which I reported everything I had been doing. I thought it was unusual because I hadn't written any of it. That, however, was just one further bizarre ingredient in a very bizarre story, which for me ended when I flew from Belfast to Prestwick and then drove on to Ayr to present the Saturday afternoon racing on *World of Sport*. It was good to get back to normal.

Shergar was never found and nobody except the kidnappers really knows for sure what happened to him. Some of the suggestions are extremely gruesome and, if correct, it is shocking that such a wonderful, gentle and trusting horse should have met such an horrific end. All but one of the shareholders, Shergar's vet

Stan Cosgrove, had their insurance claims paid out, but it transpired that none of the shareholders ever intended to pay a penny to the negotiators. They felt that had they done so a dangerous precedent would have been set. They could not have been seen to deal with the IRA, which, of course, made a fatal mistake. They forgot that the Irish are a horse-loving people. Even hard republican sympathisers were angered by what the IRA had done. It had brought shame on the nation and done nothing for its cause.

I would so love to know what really happened. Whenever I go to Ireland I get asked about Shergar. My own personal hunch is that he was taken by boat from the country's south coast, but like everyone else, I just don't know. I am, however, certain that the person I was speaking to on the phone was directly linked to the kidnap. The third codename he gave me was 'King Neptune'. Many years later, the IRA supergrass Sean O'Callaghan wrote in a book that the organisation had indeed been responsible for the Shergar kidnap. One of the codenames he used was 'King Neptune'. That convinces me I had been dealing with one of the real kidnappers.

Whether I was or was not, there is one thing that disappoints me. The Aga Khan never thanked me, and as far as I'm aware he never thanked John or Peter, either, for trying to help in the rescue of his horse. None of the shareholders did. Yet that is not the thing that disappoints me most. The greatest sadness is that Shergar was never seen again. The horse I had been in awe of at Epsom disappeared without a trace. The mystery will surely never be solved, but for good reasons as well as bad, nor will Shergar's name ever be forgotten.

TWELVE

TALKING ABOUT OLYMPIANS WITH PEGS ON THEIR NOSES

D uring my time on *World of Sport* the programme began to enter its dying days. I would like to think that one did not cause the other.

For years part of the programme's appeal had been the weird and wacky variety of sports that it showcased. True, what you watched might not have been top-notch action every single Saturday, but there was a place for international log rolling, and that place was on ITV on a Saturday afternoon. Unfortunately, what had once attracted viewers to *World of Sport* eventually turned them off it. *Grandstand* remained in its pomp for a further two decades but *World of Sport* would meet its maker on a late September afternoon in 1985.

By the time *World of Sport* ended, ITV had already got rid of some of its racing coverage. In 1984 it decided that midweek racing was no longer pulling in enough ratings to justify its place in the schedules. However, ITV could not simply just drop the sport. It was contractually obliged to cover certain meetings, so to get around the problem it offered its midweek fixtures to the fledgling Channel 4, which jumped at the chance to pick up a major live sport. ITV continued producing the Channel 4 output and viewers saw exactly the same team on their screen. It must have seemed a little odd. Two weeks before the last rites on *World of Sport* were read, Channel 4 televised the first three days of Doncaster's St Leger meeting but the Leger itself was shown as part of *World of Sport* on ITV. By that point we knew that ITV no longer had any desire to cover racing and from October 1985 all racing on commercial television switched to Channel 4, which approached the sport with a relish and enthusiasm that had long since faded at ITV.

But nobody can deny that racing owed ITV a tremendous debt of gratitude as so many fans of the sport got a significant portion of their regular fix from watching *World of Sport* or ITV's midweek coverage. For many years ITV was the home of not just the Derby but all the Classics. It was ITV that showed Shergar winning the Derby and it was ITV that showed Brigadier Gerard beating Mill Reef and My Swallow in one of the greatest of all 2,000 Guineas. It was also ITV that showed the Redcar meeting on 28 September 1985, when the track became the last racecourse to feature on *World of Sport*. Perhaps rightly, and as an indication of ITV's lost love, this was no ITV Seven or ITV Six but an ITV Three with just a trio of races being shown from my old local course. It was nice to be the presenter that day, but it was also a bit upsetting to know that the programme we were on was sinking while we were on it.

Perhaps one of the reasons why it did sink was that *World of Sport* never really changed. The racing coverage reflected that failure to move with the times. When I was presenting from a track I would be sitting behind the same desk that Ken Butler had sat at 20 years earlier. The way we did it remained link to me, horses in vision, over to the commentator, back to me for a replay of the closing stages and then back to Dickie or Brough. I spent five years on *World of Sport* largely sat behind a desk and it is my firm opinion that sitting behind a desk is boring for both viewers and those they are viewing.

But at times *World of Sport* could be anything but boring, certainly for those who worked on it. At its best, it had an inspiring attitude. It wanted to entertain the watching public. For that reason when racing was abandoned at one of the ITV Saturday tracks we often made sure that we still showed racing, albeit with dogs not horses. These days when the scheduled turf meetings are abandoned, *Channel 4 Racing* just picks up all-weather action instead. When *World of Sport* was alive all-weather racing did not exist, so if our meetings were lost, obviously most often in the winter, we would attempt to send our cameras to the greyhound racing at Hackney, Harringay or sometimes both. I don't think either Brough Scott or myself are greyhound racing experts – in fact I know next to nothing about the sport except that the hare is usually first past the post – but we still often found ourselves at one of the London tracks, generally accompanied by Raleigh Gilbert, to cover three dog races.

Not that our greyhound racing commentator was always a member of the racing team. Reg Gutteridge, ITV's voice of boxing, was also on occasions ITV's voice of the dogs, although on one Saturday afternoon he was the voice of both. Sometimes *World of Sport* had to be done ever so slightly on the cheap. This was very evident on a cold winter Saturday when I had been diverted to Harringay after our planned racing was lost to the weather. Reg was there to call the races, which he duly did as immaculately as ever. After I had done my final link back to the studio, I heard Dickie Davies talking in my ear. He was telling the viewers that they were now going to show the previous week-end's big fight from Las Vegas, at which he said Reg had been ringside for ITV. That's odd, I thought. I'd been speaking to Reg in between races and he told me he'd spent the previous weekend at home. When the pictures started there was no sound. Nothing at all. The pictures went back to Dickie, who apologised for the technical problem. The next noise I heard was a loud tap-tap-tapping on the floor. I turned round to see Reg, who had a peg leg, dashing from the toilet back to our broadcast position.

'Out of the way Tommo,' he said and then after he had sat down, he put on his headphones, picked up his microphone, and said: 'Hello, ladies and gentlemen, this is Reg Gutteridge, speaking to you from Las Vegas.'

That particular night, Las Vegas bore a striking resemblance to Harringay dog track.

The end of *World of Sport* did not mean the end of my time on ITV. Thanks to ITV I got to attend the 1988 Olympic Games in Seoul, although that wasn't my first time at a summer games. I can go to my grave saying that I was three times an Olympian. Moreover, unlike the vast majority of Olympians, I represented a different team every time I performed.

My Olympic debut came in 1980 when I was sent by the BBC to Moscow as part of the corporation's radio squad. What an experience that was. I've always been an avid fan of most sports, so to be paid to cover the greatest of all sporting competitions was something else. In theory, my duties in Moscow centred on the equestrian events. I did quite a bit of that for the BBC and was often at the Horse of the Year Show or Royal International Horse Show, which meant I already knew plenty of the people connected to the equestrian disciplines.

Right from the start Moscow was memorable. I managed to get hold of a ticket for the opening ceremony, which is something I won't forget. Nor will I forget being in the main stadium when Seb Coe exacted revenge on Steve Ovett, who had beaten him in the 800 metres final, by winning the 1,500 metres final. Both men had been favourites for the races in which they were turned over, so the drama connected to their head-to-heads was intense. To make being there even more special, I got Seb's autograph. He didn't ask for mine. This was also an Olympics when Daley Thompson took gold for Great Britain in the decathlon, which perhaps explains why this D Thompson was able to get into the big athletics events so often! What a wonderful coincidence. Perhaps he's spent some of the subsequent years being called Tommo.

If I'm being completely honest, and apologies here to any Russian racing fans who might be reading this, I didn't really warm to Moscow, although I'm sure it has since changed as its politics have progressed in the right direction. This was a dicey enough time, and of course it was famously a games that was marred by multiple boycotts, most notably by the USA. I've always tried not to get too closely involved in politics, but I did find Moscow an unsettling place. The USSR, as it was then, felt like a closed country. Nobody went there. Everywhere you looked there were sinister-looking policemen. It was actually quite frightening and it certainly wasn't a place in which you wanted to find yourself stranded, which on two occasions I did.

The first time came when I missed the press bus back to the city centre. There wasn't a taxi in sight and everybody I tried to ask for help seemed to speak Russian. Heaven knows what would have happened to me had I not been picked up by some friends from the Irish state broadcaster RTE.

My second hairy moment came as a result of my own silliness. One of our female interpreters had rather caught my eye and so I asked her if she would like to come for a drink in my room. She did, but within 30 seconds of her arriving there was a loud knock at the door and a large ugly security guard let it be known very firmly that women were not allowed in the rooms. Being a gent I offered to take her home. By the time we got there it was about three o'clock in the morning. I asked her if it would be possible for me to come in. She said no and closed the door in my face. Not having the best of bearings I then got lost trying to find the hotel. I saw a guy asleep in a taxi and asked if he could take me to my hotel but he couldn't speak English so I had no way of communicating with him. That was a truly terrible night.

In terms of my work in Moscow, it was mostly uneventful. Because of all the boycotts only 11 teams competed in the equestrian events and it was even less interesting to the listeners back home as there was no British representation. What I do remember is that it was quite difficult for me because so many of the foreign riders had tricky names, including the showjumping gold medallist Jan Kowalczyk, who beat a Mr Nikolai Korolkov into second.

A much easier name to pronounce was Neil Adams, although I hadn't been expecting to have to pronounce it. I was in the hotel on a day off when I got a phone call from one of the producers telling me I was needed at the judo in half an hour as Neil Adams was going for gold.

'Who is Neil Adams?', I asked. I might well have asked what is judo because I knew nothing about it. I was given the telephone number of a judo expert back home and on the way to the Central Lenin Stadium, where the fights were taking place, he filled me in on a few facts about Neil. Even so, as I sat in the stadium I still felt a wee bit clueless. It was so boring as well. It was just one man throwing another man to the ground. For most of the time I didn't know what to say. I do remember regularly using the line: 'He's got him by the lapels!' I also remember that saying that made me laugh on air quite a lot. Poor old Neil didn't win and ended up with silver, but I believe he then started dating the lovely swimmer Sharron Davies for a while, so the 1980s weren't totally disappointing for him.

Neil also took silver four years later in Los Angeles but I was unable to join him. I had been booked to be part of ITV's team in America only for ITV to pull out of the games two weeks before they were due to start. This sounds daft but they had suddenly realised how expensive it was going to be to cover so they left the BBC to do it alone. In reality, ITV was never in love with the Olympics and they bowed out for the final time in 1988, when I was part of the team in Seoul. Channel 4 had given me permission to go there, although that was made easier by the fact that ITV was sharing coverage with Channel 4 in a bid to make the mission more cost-effective.

If we are being completely honest, an Olympic Games is something people prefer to watch on the BBC and it was always going to be hard for us to compete with the Beeb's team, headed up by my old mate Des Lynam. The ITV/Channel 4 attack was fronted by, somewhat bizarrely, the BBC's film critic Barry Norman and Nick Owen, who normally worked on breakfast television with Anne Diamond and Roland Rat but for the Olympics had to make do without them. Barry and Nick stayed in London but I was flown out to South Korea. That said, I almost missed the flight having dashed from Doncaster, where I was working for Channel 4 at the St Leger.

Seoul was a much more enjoyable place to be than Moscow but it was also somewhere that you never felt 100 per cent secure. There was a huge underground shopping arcade that was deemed to be a safe place to be if the North Koreans ever invaded. There also wasn't a corridor longer than 50 yards because they reckoned it would be harder for a North Korean to get close enough to shoot you if there wasn't a firing line more than 50 yards long. It was one of the most incredible things I've seen in my life. Luckily nobody tried to shoot me.

As in Moscow I was assigned to be the principal commentator for the equestrian events, which was smashing as we did very well that year. Our three-day event team won silver medals and individually we got silver and bronze through Ian Stark and Virginia Leng. I thought Virginia, or Ginny as she was known, was adorable and she very kindly allowed me to take her out one night for dinner. Unfortunately she insisted that her mother had to come along as well, so I brought ITV's head of sport John Bromley to keep Ginny's mother entertained. We had a really enjoyable night, but it was a late one – how Ginny managed to ride the next day I'll never know! She did, though, and returned home with two medals. I recall there being some sort of problem when I interviewed her along with her three team-mates after the medal ceremony. Mark Phillips apparently was heard to say something that sounded a bit rude but I couldn't tell what it was so we just carried on regardless.

As in Moscow, I was called up to do more than showjumping in Seoul. From out of the blue I was asked to go to the pool and commentate on synchronised swimming. I knew even less about synchronised swimming than I'd known about judo. I rang Bob Champion and asked for some advice. He told me to go to the library and find a book on synchronised swimming, but when I got there none of the books was in English. It was no help whatsoever. I managed to get through it, and America and Canada did best so the swimmers' names weren't too much of a problem, but you can only make so many jokes about ladies wearing pegs on their noses.

Pleasingly, the Seoul Olympics proved quite lucrative for me. Seoul was a place where you could get any item of clothing made up at very short notice – and very cheaply as well. It dawned on me that replicas of the British team's tracksuit would be popular, so I had 56 made at £10 each. They were very good as well. I sold them all to members of the ITV team as mementos at £15 each. That was wonderful.

Also wonderful was being involved in the 1992 Barcelona Olympics, although I wasn't based in Spain but France. Eurosport had asked me to provide commentary on the synchronised swimming – again! – but they had the commentaries done from their own studios in Paris. I suppose that made it an odd Olympic experience but it was more pleasurable because I took my wife-to-be Julie with me. I'd managed to forget everything I'd learnt about synchronised swimming, apart from the pegs, but I was clever this time. I sat in front of the monitor with Julie alongside me holding a book about synchronised swimming. It worked brilliantly. As one of the ladies went under water Julie would point to a picture in the book and I'd say something like: 'Wow, what a superb side fishtail. That was outstanding!' It turns out that if you mention the phrases bent knee, split position and ballet leg often enough you can get by as a credible synchronised swimming commentator. And even when things are going slowly, you can go back to the pegs on the noses.

Sadly, since Barcelona I've not been involved in an Olympics, although I'm always available. I have, however, had an influence on the BBC's coverage of the Olympics. Now this is a great story. In the 1980s, in a bid to boost my somewhat insubstantial ITV income, I started a company called Derek Thompson Associates. I had always wanted to get into the public relations world and after meeting a PR expert called Anne White that's what I did. Anne had a basement office in the West End but the business wasn't going well, so she invited me to get involved. Derek Thompson Associates was born.

The story behind my proudest achievement in the PR world has never been told – until now. One morning Anne got a phone call from a young lady who was keen to speak to me. I had met the lady once before and found her charming. She was also very famous. She had just retired from a highly successful sporting career and wanted my advice on what she should do next. She asked if she could come and see me, which she did, and over a very enjoyable meeting I told her she would be highly sought after in television if she decided to head in that direction. I told her who she should write to and what her strategy needed to be. And do you know what? The advice paid off.

That lady was none other than Sue Barker. I'm so proud of her. We still talk about it to this day and I had a smashing time with her recently reminiscing in a wine bar. You would struggle to meet a lovelier or more genuine lady than Sue and, of course, she got involved in racing as well by presenting the Grand National, Derby and Arc for the BBC. Sadly she stopped doing that, but it was racing's loss. She remains a major star at the Beeb and I thought she was as fantastic as ever during London 2012 and then this year when hosting coverage of Andy Murray's historic victory at Wimbledon.

How Cliff Richard let Sue slip through his fingers I'll never know. Fortunately, she met the man of her dreams, a guy with the wonderful name Lance Tankard, and they live together happily in a huge Surrey mansion with a group of Rottweilers.

I might not have been working there, for my time as an Olympian is sadly over, but when I watched Sue presenting the main BBC programmes in London, I thought that in some small way Tommo was still involved in the Olympic Games.

THIRTEEN

JANIE

I can still remember what Janie McLaren was wearing the first time I met her. There was a beautiful light blue sweater and a pair of extremely smart jeans on a girl who was even more striking than her clothes. She had the most wonderful blonde hair, long legs, balletic arms and stunning eyes. To my dying day I will carry in my head that image. It will not fade but nor will another image fade. This one is of Janie a little over 20 years later, lying in a hospital bed, a pale imitation of what she had once been, her body savaged by cancer at its most wicked. In the time sandwiched by those two images, Janie and I had married, produced two children and divorced. Then she had become horribly ill, taking an unstoppable descent into desperate sickness for which some in her family blamed me then and very probably still blame me now. They might be right. Nobody will ever know, but what nobody will ever know more than me is my sadness and regret at the way my relationship with Janie McLaren deteriorated.

When I first met Janie we were both employees of the BBC in the late 1970s. She was a studio manager, while I was still a member of the BBC Radio sports team. I was recording a piece one day when she caught my eye. She was gorgeous but I had never seen her before and knew nothing about her. I did a bit of digging and spoke to one of the secretaries in the office who I had discovered was her best friend. I arranged a meeting, we chatted for a while and arranged to go out for a drink. I said I would pick her up from her home in Teddington, where she was staying with her sister and brother-in-law. Therein, however, was a problem.

'That's not a good idea,' she told me before explaining why.

Janie was Scottish, albeit only just. Her father was the legendary BBC rugby union commentator Bill McLaren. Whatever fame I later managed as a racing broadcaster was light years behind what Bill achieved in his own career behind the microphone. He was the voice of his sport, a figure right up there with the likes of Peter O'Sullevan, Dan Maskell and David Coleman. In rugby circles he was revered and for good reason, for he was magnificent at his job. Along with his devoted wife Bette he lived in Hawick in the Scottish borders. England was practically within touching distance from their home but the McLarens could not have been more Scottish.

Certain members of the family were fiercely patriotic and revelled in Scotland's sporting rivalry with England. Janie's sister Linda and her husband Alan Lawson, a successful rugby union player, lived in Teddington, Surrey, which was very much in England, but Janie thought it best for me not to pick her up from their house. The shock of an Englishman taking Janie out might have been a bit much for her sister! I said I would go along with whatever Janie wanted, so we met outside the small Tesco supermarket in Teddington. From there I took Janie back to my home in Walton on Thames and cooked her a meal. She couldn't stay late as she was working a night shift at the BBC's Bush House, so I drove her back to the local station, told her how much I'd enjoyed our evening together and asked if she would like to do it again. She said she would. Soon enough we were an item.

A few months after we started dating Janie invited me to Murrayfield to watch the Calcutta Cup game between Scotland and England in what was then the Five Nations championship. She suggested we get there early so she could finally introduce me to Linda and Alan, who himself had played a few games for Scotland as scrum half. We all met in the Murrayfield car park and after exchanging pleasantries I said to Linda: 'May the best team win.' That didn't go down well. She made very clear that regardless of who won or lost, the best team was Scotland. As Janie and I walked away I expressed surprise at quite how partisan Linda seemed to be. I have to admit it worried me slightly.

To be fair to Bill, or Papa as we called him, he was always perfectly friendly towards me. I had enormous respect for him as a broadcaster and as a person but I also have no doubt that Bill, Bette and Linda would have been so much happier had Janie been seeing a Scotsman. But they adored her and so went along with what she was doing – even when she married her chosen Englishman in 1980.

It maybe helped that we were married in Scotland and also that we produced two new McLarens, our sons Alex, born in 1982, and James, who arrived into the world two years later. Both boys were born in Catterick as Janie and I had moved to Bedale in North

Yorkshire after marrying, principally because so many of my *World of Sport* racecourse shifts were at northern tracks. After a while we all moved south to Chalfont St Giles in Buckinghamshire, which was closer to London, where my PR agency was starting to take up more of my time. It also made sense as once Channel 4 took over from ITV as the broadcaster of racing on commercial television there were initially far fewer second site meetings in the schedule and so much more of my work was at southern venues. Relocating to the south of England suited everyone, except the McLarens, who no doubt noted that their daughter was now living even further from Scotland.

Not for a second would I claim that Janie was ever anything other than a fantastic wife. She had her independence because she retrained as an aerobics instructor and proved very successful. With me working many more hours than I should have done, she took on much more than 50 per cent of the responsibilities in the raising of Alex and James. The boys could not have had a better mother and I could not have had a better wife. Unfortunately I messed things up.

There is no point me pretending that some good did not come of the collapse of my marriage to Janie. I am now married to Julie, a quite exceptional woman, and together we have two superb children in India and Hugo. But to get to that stage was anything but easy and I am not proud of some of my behaviour along the way.

At the point when things started to go wrong there were no indications that we had a problem. In fact we didn't have a problem. My first marriage to Jenny had failed disastrously and I was aware that I had to try harder to make things work. I'm a natural flirt, partly because I like talking to people, which as a television presenter goes with the job. There were occasions when I flirted a little too much, such as with the Russian interpreter during the Moscow Olympics, but I don't think I was a terrible husband. My problem stemmed from the fact that I was blown away by the sight of Julie Corney when I saw the local lass for the first time at Doncaster on the opening day of the 1988 St Leger festival.

I was interviewing a jockey when Julie walked past in my eye line. I was deeply impressed. I pointed out the amazing lady I'd seen to Brough Scott, who was stood next to me at the time. He agreed that she was very beautiful so my eyes clearly were not deceiving me. I was desperate to ask her out but I could hardly do that while I was broadcasting to a million people on Channel 4. This might sound a little strange – although I've done a few strange things over the years – but I asked my floor manager Mark Hinchcliffe if he would pass a little note to Julie. It's an unusual request to make of a floor manager, but Mark, although a tad bemused, agreed. I wrote a few words on the note and asked the mysterious girl if she would allow me to take her out to dinner. Mark passed her the note, the girl read it and then gave her response to Mark. The answer was no. Apparently asking a lady out via a note passed to your floor manager was not deemed to be the right way to do things. (Coincidentally Mark would later attain a celebrity in-law of his own when his sister Gill married her long-term partner Sir David 'Del Boy' Jason. Sadly Mark was, like me, one of those who lost out when Channel 4 moved their production contract from Highflyer to IMG in 2013.)

One of my qualities has always been persistence, so I did my best to keep track of the movements of Julie, who was at the races with an older lady that turned out to be her mother, Mary Summerfield. After we finished the programme I had a second attempt at securing a date, but this time I kept Mark out of it and approached Julie myself. She thought I was the BBC's snooker, showjumping and *Ski Sunday* presenter David Vine. I explained I wasn't, told her who I actually was, and this time she agreed. That night we enjoyed a lovely dinner together. Before we did, she rang her dad, Syd, and told him that she was having a meal that night with a member of the *Channel 4 Racing* team. His reaction did not bode well. Apparently he said that he just hoped it wasn't 'that buffoon Derek Thompson'! For some reason whenever I came on TV he turned down the sound. Bizarre.

My main concern was that Julie liked me, so it was important that dinner went well. It did. When we got to the restaurant we were sat down at the very next table to the jockey Joe Mercer. The first thing Joe said to Julie when he saw us was: 'You haven't got a sister, have you?' I thought that was very funny.

The following day there was interest from certain members of the Channel 4 team as to how the date had gone, not least from John Francome, who has always been such a winner with the ladies. I told Francs that the evening had passed off very well indeed and that I had arranged to see Julie again the following night. Francs then suggested he come with us. It must have seemed a good idea at the time, but I'm not sure it did to John when he discovered what we were planning to do on the date. Julie has always been keen on keeping fit and on a Friday night often went to an aerobics class. I had arranged to go along with her. The advantages of joining her in the class were obvious. It would make for a fun, relaxed evening and clearly it wouldn't cost a lot, either. And I was right! I loved it. I got into the spirit of things, putting on a leotard-like outfit and joining in with all the moves. I actually think I was quite good at it, but the same was not true of John, who for a nimble guy was surprisingly useless. I'm also pleased to report that this was the last time the three of us went out on a date together. However, Julie, like most women, has always remained extremely fond of Francs. Quite how fond I did begin to wonder one Saturday. Julie had put our baby son Hugo in front of the television when *The Morning Line* started. She told him to shout and wave when he saw his daddy. Julie says that he sat there quiet as a church mouse throughout my opening bit but then as soon as Francs appeared in shot he started screaming: 'Daddy, daddy!'

Worryingly, Hugo has curly hair.

On those two Doncaster dates with Julie nothing happened that was any more sordid than a bit of flirting. Even so, I knew I had done wrong and I had plenty of time to think about it because as soon as the St Leger programme finished on the Saturday I was hurtling down south to Gatwick to catch my flight to Seoul for the Olympic Games, which I was working on for ITV. When the games were over I flew on to Hong Kong, where Janie met up with me and we began a smashing holiday that took us on to Bangkok. I had never at any point fallen out of love with Janie and our holiday together only reminded me of the fact. When we got home I rang Julie and explained how I felt. I was in a very difficult situation, but so was Julie, as she was married at the time to a surgeon. We both knew that an affair would have been very silly and dangerous so we agreed that it was best if we did not see each other again. But then, a few weeks later, I was working at Doncaster's November Handicap meeting. I rang Julie and asked her out for a coffee. From there things developed quite rapidly.

There is no excuse for what I did. This will sound deeply hypo–critical but in many ways I'm rather old-fashioned. I knew what I was doing was wrong and I felt horribly guilty. Janie was every bit as wonderful as the day I had fallen in love with her, but I had also now fallen in love with Julie. I wanted to be with Julie but it was not fair on her to continue as we were, and it certainly wasn't fair on Janie. So six months into the affair I sat Janie down at home and made a full and frank confession.

I have a tendency to make myself believe what I want to believe. Foolishly I had somehow convinced myself that Janie would in some way understand my predicament. I began my little speech clinging to the hope she would forgive me and that the three of us would manage to find a way forward that could work for us all. I was stupid and naive to think that. Why on earth would Janie, the mother of my two children, have under-stood her husband's betrayal? She did not. She took the news incredibly badly. I felt so very sorry for her. There were faults on both sides, but on mine more than hers, and she had not deserved any of the sadness I had just heaped on her shoulders. In the end, she decided that she had to leave me. Not surpris-ingly she returned to her family in Scotland. Another memory that will always stay with me is the one of Janie, Alex and James disappearing into the distance in her brand new red Ford Escort. As the car pulled away I could see Alex and James waving at me from the back seat. It is a mark of Janie McLaren's goodness and decency that at no point did she ever attempt to turn her children against their father. She was furious with me but did not convey that fury to the boys. Throughout the whole sad and sorry mess Janie never questioned my love for our sons.

Janie had gone and I wanted to be with Julie. She told her husband that she was in love with another man. Janie and I had already agreed that we should sell the house so Julie and I were never going to live together there. We discussed where we should make a home together. Julie hit on the idea of moving to Newmarket, the home of Flat racing. For a number of work reasons it made good sense for me to live there and I also had my best mate in the town as Bob Champion had bought a lovely place in Newmarket, too. Bob had started a new career as a trainer, and would continue as a trainer until 1999. He said I could stay in a small house he had on his property while Julie and I looked for somewhere of our own. I had to share with a slightly unpleasant girl who was also living in the house but Bob's kindness gave me some breathing space and also somewhere for Julie to see me when she came down to pay visits. It was a difficult time, not least because the breakdown of my marriage had caught the interest of some tabloid journalists, but I knew that I had only myself to blame. This was one I had to take on the chin.

Julie and I found a place, bought it and moved in. We have lived together ever since, but while being with Julie made me exceptionally happy, I was apart from my kids, which made me exceptionally sad. Janie had found a new home and a new job in Edinburgh and was keen for me to see the children at weekends, but I worked almost every Saturday for Channel 4, so getting up to Scotland on a regular basis was difficult, and even more so because, not surprisingly, Julie was not wildly enthusiastic about me leaving her every weekend. I worked as hard as ever and ensured the children attended top-notch private schools, but while I provided money I did not provide them with a father. The occasions when I was able to see them were always special and I recall bursting into tears when I watched them competing at their school sports day.

Janie and I divorced in 1992. Julie and I got engaged two years later and were married in 1996, far later than Julie would have liked. It had become a constant source of frustration that I was reluctant to get down on one knee and propose. Perfectly understandably I'd like to think, I was not overly keen to enter into marriage for a third time, especially as we seemed to be getting on so well just cohabiting. We had a flat at the bottom of Warren Hill, which meant I was able to stand on the balcony in my pyjamas watching the horses work while Julie, who was effectively my assistant as well as my partner, kept up a steady supply of my morning favourites, coffee and chocolate croissants. The crunch came thanks to the Manchester United and England footballer Bryan Robson. I was interviewing him on Newmarket's July course when he asked me live on air when I planned to marry Julie! What I didn't know is that the pair of them had been talking and plotting before the interview started. That forced my hand somewhat, but even after I did eventually ask her to marry me I kept procrastinating and putting off the wedding. That said, I wasn't short of romanticism and bought a horse with two friends that I named in recognition of my engagement to Julie. I called the filly Capture The Moment and to our delight she was good enough to run at Royal Ascot in 1995, although she could only manage 12th as a 50-1 shot in the Windsor Castle Stakes under my good friend Richard Hills.

In June 1996 we finally did tie the knot. Hoping for a change of luck I got Willie Ryan, the following year's Derby-winning jockey and for so long the number-two rider to Henry Cecil, to take over from Bob as best man. More than 250 people came to the wedding and it was an outstanding occasion. It had taken a little longer than Julie had hoped, but the two of us had cemented our future together. Tragically, Janie's future was soon to be cut short.

Part of me thinks that I was responsible for Janie's cancer. Part of me always will. Generally I can keep the thought at the back of my mind, tucked away and hidden with all the other things I don't like to think about, but then there are nights when I open my eyes at 3am and think to myself: 'Christ, was it me?'

Common sense tells you it could not really have been due to me, but sometimes, when you're feeling at your most emotional, vulnerable or guilty, common sense makes no sense. In 1997 Janie was diagnosed with skin cancer. Two lumps had appeared on her back, which, when removed, were found to be malignant melanoma. A year later, in March 1998, she was discovered slumped at the steering wheel of her car. She had collapsed on the way to an appointment with her doctor but had just about managed to bring the car to a halt. When she got to Edinburgh Royal Infirmary she was given the terrible news that she had a brain tumour. As if that wasn't enough the cancer had spread to her chest and lungs. She was given no more than a year to live but Janie was a fighter from top to toe and she fought, adamant that she wanted to spend every possible day she could with Alex and James, who by that point were teenagers and had been living with their mum in Edinburgh since we separated. The tumour was removed and Janie began a course of chemotherapy in the hope that the drugs might kill off the cancer. That did not prove possible.

By April 2000 it was obvious that the end was close. In the weeks and months leading up to her death it was made very clear to me that some of the McLarens blamed me for what was happening to Janie. There is a theory that stress can be a contributing factor in the acquirement of cancer and there is no doubt that I caused Janie considerable stress. We had spent far too much time arguing after I admitted to the affair and our separation and subsequent divorce had hit her very badly. That was not all, though. One Christmas while we were living in Yorkshire I had bought Janie a sunbed as a present. In those days people just didn't think about the damaging effect they could have. Maybe the sunbed did induce some of Janie's problems. If so, a degree of the blame again falls to me. Another factor might have been that when she was younger Janie spent a lot of summers under blazing sunshine in Greece. She loved it there, but those regular trips might not have done her any good. We just don't know and we never will.

When I was told she was really struggling I flew up to see her in hospital. Linda was there and was being very civil at the time. She told me that Janie was now extremely ill. I told her not to worry. I said I would cheer her up. What a fool I was. Janie had been a blonde bombshell, a beautiful person inside and out. Through a window I looked at her lying in bed and saw a different person. She looked about 90 years old. The weight had fallen off her. She could not have been more than seven stone. I was genuinely stunned.

I couldn't go in. I couldn't face it. I was too much of a coward. A nurse asked me if I wanted a cup of tea, which I gratefully accepted because tea helps at times like that. Except that it doesn't. Not really. It's just something that briefly takes your mind away from the something you don't want to think about. I spent about half an hour only a few feet away from Janie but without her knowing I was there. After those 30 minutes had gone I realised I had to go in. It was obvious this could be my last chance. I owed her. I loved her.

For about four hours I just lay next to her on the bed. I put an arm around her and she put an arm around me. She could hardly move. Life had been sucked out of this vibrant, fun-loving woman, the girl who had dazzled me in her light blue sweater back at the BBC all those years ago. So much had changed since then. None of it I could make right, least of all this. Two days later she died.

When she died that Saturday afternoon I was in Newmarket. Bill was also absent, but only because Janie had ordered him to fulfil his commentary duties at the Scottish cup final. I had returned south as Julie had organised a charity ball at which I was master of ceremonies. I got the phone call late in the afternoon after Julie had set off to get the marquee organised. Janie was dead. I was in Newmarket. My two boys were in Edinburgh, without their dad. And then I did what I had to do and what Tommo always does. I performed. I was the host with the most, smiles, jokes, 'ho, ho hos' and 'hey big fellas'. For a few hours Janie's death became the latest thing to be forced into a recess deep in the back of my mind. That time it was difficult.

The following morning I flew to Scotland and saw the kids. Alex and James were only 18 and 15. Their mother had been just 46 when she died. I took mum with me to provide me with some moral support. Somehow that seems ironic. To get me through those days I needed the one thing my sons now no longer had – a mother. We went to see Linda and Alan at their home in Dollar, near Stirling, but mum and I stayed in a hotel. That seemed only right. Linda, Alan and Bette had been there with Janie when she died but Bill felt awful that he had not been. He was resentful and he was angry. I could see completely why some of that anger should be directed at the man who had left his daughter heartbroken. To their credit, the McLarens were very good over the next two days, even Linda, who understandably has a pretty low opinion of me. She had been so very close to her sister. She worshipped the ground Janie walked on. For her, as for all the family, this was incredibly tough.

Quite rightly, the McLarens were adamant that Janie's funeral should celebrate her life. They did not want it to be a morbid, distressing experience, so they asked everyone to avoid wearing black and to come along in brightly coloured clothes. It was a fine idea, as it was to ask Alex to address the funeral. Alex spoke about his mother in the most beautiful, evocative manner and got a well-deserved round of applause from the packed congregation at Dean Church. I may never have been more proud of anyone.

Collectively we decided it was best for the boys to remain in Scotland. Alex had already reached the age where he could do what he wanted anyway and he continued his studies in Scotland. James went to live with Linda and Alan and attended the Dollar Academy before graduating from Napier University. Then my two sons began living together once again in the flat their mother had bought for them without any of us knowing she had done so at the time. Despite the tragedy that hit them at such a young age, they have grown into superb young men. Alex works very successfully in the property business and James has lived up to his breeding by becoming a rugby union player, just like his cousin, Linda and Alan's son, Rory Lawson. James, or Jim as he is known in the rugby world, spent four years playing for Edinburgh before joining London Scottish in 2012. It is the national team's loss that he has never had a full cap for Scotland.

I know that I was not always the father I should have been. I made sure the boys wanted for nothing financially, but I did not give them the time they deserved. Maybe that's why the odd possibly harmless remark sometimes hits a nerve. James recently got married to a lovely nurse called Lynsey. I had a smashing time with him at his stag do, and he introduced me to many of his team-mates, but at the reception following the ceremony it was Linda and Alan who were given places alongside the bride and groom on the top table. In his speech he thanked Linda and Alan for all they had done for him and presented them with a beautiful picture. He then said that his dad was here as well, pointed me out, thanked me for all I'd done and promised to buy me a pint.

'Right, okay,' I thought to myself. In my head his words seemed to mean something. They very possibly did and, if they did, I could hardly complain. I don't even drink pints.

I regret that I was not a better husband to Janie and I regret that I was not a better father to Alex and James. I now try doubly hard with Julie, India and Hugo, but that cannot right old wrongs. What happened to Janie was tragic, and it is a tremendous disappointment that I no longer have much of a relationship with most of the McLarens. What I do have, however, are two super sons, both great representatives of the Thompson and McLaren families. I love them dearly. Their mother would have been justifiably proud. Janie did a fine job.

FOURTEEN

CHANNEL 4: PART ONE

B y far the longest relationship of my working career was with Channel 4. It began in 1984, when ITV handed over its rights to show midweek racing, increased in 1985 when Channel 4 took on full responsibility for the televising of racing on commercial television, and ended on Boxing Day at Kempton in 2012 with me waving a final goodbye to viewers while standing behind the main front man Alastair Down. I say final goodbye because it seems highly unlikely that I shall ever again get the chance to present racing on Channel 4. We parted on sad, disappointing terms, but I adored being able to talk about the sport I love most on terrestrial television. If I ever got the chance to do it again, I'd be lying if I said I wouldn't jump at the chance.

The *Channel 4 Racing* programmes you watch today are very different to the ones I was so closely involved with when Channel 4 picked up the baton from ITV. In some ways it was a seamless link. We had the same racecourse contracts and we were largely the same team, both in front of the camera and behind it, although the team got bigger and better very quickly. At first the coverage changed in approach and we tended to concentrate on just a single meeting on Saturdays, but in time the style returned to much more like what we did on ITV, with two meetings, and sometimes even three or four, shown in a single programme. Perhaps most importantly for me, we also began broadcasting in the mornings.

It was very early in the life of *Channel 4 Racing* that *The Morning Line* was born. The whole team was sat in a room at York for the morning production meeting, during which the content and running order for the programme would always be finalised. Leading the meeting, as was almost always the case, was Andrew Franklin. Andrew provided another link to racing's past on ITV and throughout my time on both ITV and Channel 4 he was an ever-present. Andrew is an inspiration to anyone who wants to forge a career in the television industry. He loved racing and he loved television but had no family background in either. After writing a letter to ITV asking to be considered for work, he was given the job of tea boy on *World of Sport*, and from that point onwards rose rapidly through the ranks. Andrew later became one of the two key men in Highflyer Productions, which produced *Channel 4 Racing* throughout the majority of its lifetime and, with absolute sincerity, I can say that I have never worked for a finer producer. Until his final day in the job, which was one raceday after my final day in the job, he was devoted to *Channel 4 Racing*. Crucially, though, Andrew did not want to just make *Channel 4 Racing* better but also racing as a whole and, as a superb ideas man, he was well placed to do so. I'd like to think that Andrew and I were two peas from the same pod. Both of us positively ooze enthusiasm.

Racing owes Andrew an enormous favour. *Channel 4 Racing* brought new people into the sport and, in my humble opinion, made the sport more enjoyable to watch than ever before. He was open-minded, creative and innovative, with one of the best examples of those qualities being *The Morning Line*.

At the end of that York production meeting Andrew told us that Channel 4 had been in touch with him and had asked for a 20-minute racing programme on five consecutive Saturdays during the summer holidays. He asked what we thought it should be called and, quick as a flash, John McCririck said: 'The Morning Line'. Although British to the core, Mac adores America and had just come back from one of his many holidays in the States, where the first prices put up for a race are described as the morning line odds. 'Great idea,' said Andrew and *The Morning Line* was born. Andrew told me that I would be the presenter. I would be the presenter for very many years to come.

It did not take long for *The Morning Line* to be established as an integral part of the *Channel 4 Racing* family. For racing and for Channel 4 it proved a blessing, as not only was it a one-hour (for that's what it quickly became) magazine show for the sport, but it also helped to promote our afternoon racing coverage. We previewed the major races we would be covering and brought special racing guests on to the show. Sometimes the guests were not directly linked to racing and when, for example, we were at Sandown for Variety Club day, we had people like Jimmy Tarbuck or Bobby Davro on the programme. I loved that. We wanted the programme to appeal outside the core community of racing viewers because we knew that would bring new people to the sport and to the programmes. To make it more accessible,

Mac always did a review of the Saturday morning papers, which sometimes had the potential to be very funny due to Mac's somewhat entrenched opinions. Mac was a big character, but so many of us on *The Morning Line* were the same. That made for punchy conversations and humour that seemed to appeal to what was a pretty large audience for a show that in those days ran from 9am to 10am.

Sometimes critics said *The Morning Line*, and even the afternoon programme, were not serious enough, but to me that was rubbish. Yes, we introduced things like the Picture Puzzle, in which an artist drew a cartoon image of one of the afternoon's runners whose identity the viewers had to guess, but there is a difference between making something entertaining and dumbing it down. We had as our main afternoon presenter Brough Scott, one of the most formidable racing journalists of his era. Likewise, John Oaksey was an outstanding and hugely respected writer, while Mac also had a fully deserved reputation for being one of the sport's best campaigning journalists. All three had won awards for their work. All three had a fun side to their characters, but all three also had a deep respect for racing. We tried to mix the serious with the fun. We wanted the programmes we put out to be entertaining and informative to watch. I think they were, even the edition of *The Morning Line* in which John Francome quite audibly called me 'a tosser'. We'd been talking about cricket at the time, but even so, I'm not sure it was appropriate – and nor, of course, accurate.

The programmes we delivered were also plentiful. We were on air every Saturday morning and afternoon plus regularly during the week as well. These days Channel 4 shows racing 84 days a year but through the late 1980s and 1990s we were far busier. Channel 4 showed all five British Classics. That was a big deal to us, to the extent that Brough often referred to us as 'the Classic channel'. In fact on the Flat we were in a very strong position as domestically we held exclusive contracts to the likes of Newmarket, York, Sandown, Epsom and Doncaster. But we did not only stay in Britain. We showed most of Ireland's biggest races and for a few years also covered the Breeders' Cup. Sadly, I didn't get to go out to America for what are billed as the world championships of racing, but Brough and commentator Graham Goode would fly to the States and sometimes present one of the races live with highlights of the rest in a late-night programme. That was a great thing for us to have, but in some ways the jewel of our crown was the Prix de l'Arc de Triomphe, which we held from 1986 – the year of Dancing Brave's incredible triumph – to 1994 after stealing the rights off the BBC. Sadly for us, the Beeb won them back again in 1995 but Channel 4 did get one more crack at doing the race when regaining it for one year only in 2001. It's true that in the early days we weren't as strong over jumps, and when Channel 4 started our biggest National Hunt race was the King George VI Chase at Kempton, but we also had the Whitbread Gold Cup at Sandown, plus all the other major prizes from that track, and Ayr's Scottish National.

What we also had was money, seemingly, and a little ironically, much more money than the current Channel 4 team has to spend. The fact that Channel 4 was prepared to send a team to America and to then broadcast racing on a Saturday night shows how much the sport meant to the network in those days. When we did two meetings on a Saturday we would almost always have at least a presenter and commentator at both tracks, something you tend not to see now when Channel 4's number-two fixture is usually without a presenter and the commentary is just the same one heard on the racecourse. We also did days that Channel 4 no longer does. Newmarket's Craven meeting was on Channel 4, as were now axed Bank Holiday cards at Kempton, Epsom and Newcastle plus plenty of dropped midweek fixtures at Ayr, Doncaster and York. Moreover, when we did the Irish Derby we sent out a presenter and commentator, even though the BBC were doing exactly the same thing and we could have cut costs by just taking the output of RTE. We did it all because Channel 4 cared and wanted to make its racing coverage the best around. I believe it was.

In 1994 we were rewarded for that commitment when Cheltenham announced that from the start of 1995 its racing would be covered not by the BBC but by Channel 4. For us it was a monumental coup. For the BBC it was a desperate blow. In the world of television, contracts are always there to be won and lost, and a major event went the other way when the BBC took the Derby from Channel 4 in 2001. That was a shame, but I have no doubt that winning Cheltenham was a much bigger deal than losing the Derby, especially as we won Newbury from the BBC at around the same time they won Epsom from us. More than ever before, Cheltenham dominates the jumps season. Everything that comes before it is a precursor to Cheltenham. The Grand National meeting is another that has risen in importance, but to a large extent Cheltenham is where the whole of the season leads. By gaining the Festival the rest of our winter coverage took on new significance as well, particularly as we also gained all Cheltenham's other fixtures of note, most significantly what was then the Mackeson Gold Cup in November, the two-day December fixture, the traditional New Year's Day card and the Festival trials meeting in late January.

For me Cheltenham was heaven. Give me a microphone and someone to interview and I'm happy. At Cheltenham there are always lots of people and most of them seem to have plenty to say, particularly inside The Centaur, the vast indoor arena in which so many punters like to spend the day without ever seeing a horse or jockey in the flesh. Edward Gillespie, who seemed to be the managing director of Cheltenham forever, always says he built The Centaur especially for me. It's a sweet thing of him to say, and it's true that my style of interviewing went down especially well in that particular atmosphere. In fact, I was once doing a live piece in there when the thousands and thousands of people inside saw me on its enormous cinema-style screen. Gradually, but unmistakably, a sound began to fill the room. It was a chant. It got louder and louder. It could not be disguised. 'Tommo, Tommo, Tommo.' The punters were chanting my name while I was broadcasting live on Channel 4. I felt like a rock star. What a beautiful moment that was.

We also had some beautiful racing moments from Cheltenham. Our first year there was a wet but glorious one for Norman Williamson and Kim Bailey, who teamed up to win both the Champion Hurdle and Gold Cup courtesy of Alderbrook and Master Oats. In the early Channel 4 years we also had two famous hat-tricks with Istabraq winning three Champion Hurdles and Best Mate emulating Arkle by winning three Gold Cups. They were special days but then every day at Cheltenham is special.

151

But it wasn't only Cheltenham that swapped channels as Chester also came to us from the BBC, although this time because the BBC surprisingly dropped the track's May festival and its Epsom Classic trials, in no small part, I suppose, because back then the BBC did not have Epsom. Very often at Chester I got to be our main presenter. Brough could not do every meeting, and as he had other commitments, not least to the *Racing Post*, there were times when he was given leave from Channel 4. On those occasions I was promoted to the number-one spot. I loved it. For so much of my career I had been the deputy to the Prime Minister, always the bridesmaid but never the bride. In the early years of the new Channel 4 set-up my status was significantly enhanced. I was the main anchor of *The Morning Line* and I was second only to Brough in the afternoons. As such, I was present at many more of the major meetings than I had been in the past and was relishing the chance to show what I could do on a big stage.

Inevitably, not everyone was pleased that I had become omnipresent on all Channel 4's top racing occasions. For as long as I have appeared on television there has been a section of people, most of them professionally involved in racing, who have taken against me. They look down their noses at me, of that there is no doubt. They think Tommo is too populist, but they are right only in that I unashamedly want to make racing more popular. I want people who are watching me, whether on television or in the flesh, to be satisfied. I want them to get to the end of the programme, or to drive out of the racecourse, with a smile on their face. I don't spend two hours of a programme going into the intricate details of the form book but that's because I do not believe that is what the audience I'm talking to wants. That, however, is not to say that I don't know what I'm doing. Without wanting to blow my own trumpet, I know that I do. I broadcast with a natural exuberance, but just because I have a relaxed air that does not mean I am anything other than wholly professional. I am far more professional than most of the people I have worked with or see in press rooms. Whatever I'm doing, whether I'm presenting or commentating, I put in the homework. Indeed, throughout my time on Channel 4 I think the only person who could have claimed to have done as much homework as me was John McCririck. The only difference was he did it on the day. I used to do it the day before.

Nobody loves a bit of knockabout humour as much as me. I'm even happy to have the piss taken out of me. Indeed, very often I encourage it. What I will not tolerate is people questioning my professionalism. I do what I do with a smile on my face but nobody takes what they do more seriously.

It's also true that I can't imagine anybody gets as much pleasure from what they do as me, especially when I was on the *Channel 4 Racing* team – and even when I was suffering at the hands of the public. Not surprisingly that has happened now and again. One such occasion came at Chester. As everyone who loves racing knows, Chester is a tight track whose home bend and straight are nestled against the city walls. On the crown of the final turn the wall is separated from the racecourse by a steep bank that provides a very decent view for those racegoers who have a head for heights and can keep themselves balanced on seriously uneven terrain. Andrew thought it would make for good TV if I was sent over to the bank to interview some of those spending their afternoon there. You can probably guess what happened next.

My cameraman spotted a group of lads who, it has to be said, were not lacking in size. That, however, has never stopped me, and nor has seeing interviewees who might have had five or six pints of shandy. I approached the guys and started talking to them, asking if they were enjoying themselves and what they fancied for the next race. They knew who Tommo was, and they were clearly aware that I like a bit of well-natured banter, so they were a great laugh. But then something unpleasant happened. The incident began in the region of my bottom. While I was talking to one of the boys, another one of the party must have gone behind me because I experienced contact to my rear end that disturbed me greatly. Even worse, the finger that had been used to make the contact – and I have no idea whether the contact had been intended to be so intimate – then pushed me quite hard. When the force was applied I had my back to the hill. The next second I was falling down it, tumbling to the bottom like one of those balls of cheese some people roll down a hill somewhere on a Bank Holiday Monday. I can tell you that Tommo was sore that night.

Sometimes, though, the general public are rather more sympathetic. I was reminded of this one day at Sandown when we were there for the Whitbread Gold Cup. This was always an afternoon that the late Queen Mother attended – and, of course, she won it in 1984 with Special Cargo. After one particular renewal she made her way down to Sandown's lovely winner's enclosure for the prize-giving. Unfortunately, Her Majesty was having to wait because a stewards' inquiry had been called, as so often seemed to happen after this particular race. I was going into and out of the weighing room trying to get live updates on what was happening. While I was doing so I was having to rush past the royal guest, who I'd been fortunate enough to meet in the past. Maybe she remembered our meetings, because as I dashed by on one occasion she addressed her entourage and said: 'Make way for Mr Thompson. He's working.'

I loved that.

We were like a family. The *Channel 4 Racing* team was a very close-knit unit. We were the nearest thing you could find to an office on wheels. Week after week we would meet up on a different race-course, the same faces, the same friends, having the same great time.

The sense of togetherness came from the top. Andrew Franklin was not just a great producer but also a great leader. In the gallery, the name given to the truck inside which all the buttons were pressed and decisions made during each programme, he was accompanied by some superb individuals like Mark Jackson, Bob Gardam, Jane Garrod and Denise Large. They were all experts in their field. The cameramen, sound men, technicians, riggers, production staff and assistants were top notch as, I'd like to think, were the commentators, presenters and pundits. We had the same goal. We wanted to make the best possible programmes, whether we were doing Gold Cup day at Cheltenham or a double-header from Lingfield and Wolverhampton. We won a BAFTA for our work so I don't think we were too bad.

Incredibly, when you consider how many people were involved in making *Channel 4 Racing*, we got on very well indeed. I'm sure not everyone on the team absolutely adored me, and I think some might have liked to throttle me now and again, but we were essentially friends, as I discovered when I became ill with cancer and so many colleagues were quick to offer their love and support. It would be astonishing, however, if everyone I worked with at Channel 4 liked me and not everyone did.

John McCririck actively disliked me and I believe still does to this day. When we were both on air together Mac was always the ultimate professional. He would laugh at my jokes – some of them anyway – and if I lobbed him a verbal ball, he would hit one back over the net. Some of my best TV moments have come when the two of us have been jousting with each other. There was one particularly funny clip when we had just shown a feature on Val Ridgeway, a female masseuse who had worked successfully with a lot of the jockeys. I had been with the masseuse on the feature, so Mac asked me what it was that made her so good and so popular with the boys in the weighing room. Without thinking my answer fully through, I said: 'The beauty of this girl is that she will drop anything for a jockey.' Mac fell about laughing. When I realised what I'd said so did I.

But sadly, I have to tell you, the only times we spoke were when we were on air. Apart from that there was nothing. Just silence.

I genuinely don't know what went wrong in our relationship, although I think it might have been due to a disagreement about money. When I lived in London we were good pals. We would go out for dinner and drinks and had a great time. In those days, Mac was a very different character to the one he is today. Then Mac was not just a TV betting reporter but also a hard cam-paigning journalist. He had not become the larger-than-life TV persona that now turns up dressed in nothing but his underpants and demanding diet cola on *Celebrity Big Brother*. In those days we were mates. But then, suddenly, we were not. I don't think that John necessarily approved of my marriage to Julie, but if that was the case it was none of his business. Even when we were broadcasting there were hints about how he felt towards me. For many years I had telephone tipping lines, whereby people would ring up a number, on which I would have pre-recorded some suggestions for horses they might want to back. These were not always cheap to ring but nobody made anybody ring them and it was not me who set the rates at which the calls were charged. That was the responsibility of the phoneline provider. There were also lots of people who rang the Tommo Hotlines on a regular basis so they must have been pretty pleased with the product they were getting. Mac, however, despised them, and perhaps because he despised me as well once tore into the telephone tipping line industry during an edition of *The Morning Line*. To me that felt like a personal attack. He did not mention my lines by name, but if I went on Channel 4 and launched a verbal attack on fat men with big whiskers it wouldn't leave much to the imagination. I knew what Mac was getting at, just as I know the point he was making when it reached the stage where he refused to say good morning to me. After a while I gave up trying.

Most regrettably, I happened to make things worse a few years ago without even trying. For all that Mac and I don't get on, I still think he is an excellent TV performer and I believe it is Channel 4's loss that he is no longer part of its racing team. One of Mac's great qualities is his professionalism. When we were going on air at 3pm he would not just rock up at 2pm having done no homework. He knew his subject inside out and he reinforced his knowledge throughout the morning of a raceday by making copious notes in two racecards, copying information from one to the other so that he had a back-up document if one was needed. That's exactly what he was doing one morning at Kempton when I walked into the room where we were about to have our pre-programme production meeting.

'I've got the non-runners if anyone wants them,' I said.

'Hang on, hang on,' Mac said, opening out both his racecards and getting his pen nicely poised.

'In the third race,' I said, 'number one.'

'Right, good,' said Mac.

'And three.'

'And three,' repeated Mac.

'Thirteen.'

After a brief moment of confusion Mac spontaneously combusted. He complained that I had caused him to ruin both his racecards. Apparently I was an utter and complete fool. He was in a rage and behaving like a wild and extremely hairy animal. Everybody fell about laughing and if you ask anyone who was in the room at the time for a funny story about me they'll tell you that one. But I hadn't even been trying to be funny. I'd just thought that it would be nice to read out the non-runners in the style of a bingo caller.

A bingo caller is probably one of the few jobs that John Francome hasn't done. Both Julie and I adore Francs. The viewers of *Channel 4 Racing* seemed to feel the same and for very good reasons. Having been an outstanding jump jockey John became an outstanding broadcaster. We did have the odd difficult moment, such as the day at Newmarket's July festival when John had felt poorly during the morning meeting and had lamented the fact he had agreed to do a speaking job in a corporate box before racing. I helped him out by getting to the box early and doing the job for him. Sadly he didn't seem to appreciate my generosity. I also didn't appreciate his sense of humour once when the two of us were part of a tour called *That's Racing* that went up and down the country telling racing anecdotes to theatre audiences. Before one of the shows John said to me that we would get an early laugh if I asked him what he had for breakfast that morning. He told me that he would say kippers, to which I would say 'Finans', the name of a brand of kipper that was being sold at the time. His answer to that question would be: 'No, thick 'uns.' On the night itself I asked John what he had for breakfast that morning. He said cornflakes. Stitch up.

Truth be told, John stitched me up more than once. Julie was once a regular multiple winner of best dressed lady competitions and developed such a reputation in the field that she was once asked to judge one of the events at Newmarket. After Julie had finished the judging and announced the one-two-three live on Channel 4, John, who was stood next to me, suggested I ask Julie about her own outfit. 'Well,' she said. 'It's the same outfit I had on this day last year because you're too tight to buy me a new one.'

For years people asked me whether I've bought Julie a new outfit yet. And the reason they did was down to Francs.

When Highflyer lost the Channel 4 production contract at the end of 2012 John concluded that he did not want to work for the new production company, IMG, and so retired from terrestrial television. He did so at a time of his own choosing, just as Brough had done when he decided to say 'hello everyone' and then 'goodbye' on Channel 4 for the last time in 2001. Brough, who I hold very dear to my heart, was a fantastic broadcaster and was still a fantastic broadcaster. I think he retired too soon but I suppose it's better to leave when you remain on the top of your game.

Sadly, John Oaksey suffered from dementia in the later years of his life and so had not been seen on Channel 4 for some time before his death in 2012. That such a cruel and terrible affliction should come to haunt a wise and brilliant man who had done so much for so many others was tragic, but through the Injured Jockeys Fund Oaks left behind a wonderful and fitting legacy.

I'm afraid we've also lost some of my other former Channel 4 colleagues, such as the commentators Raleigh Gilbert and John Penney and dear old John Tyrrell, who used to read out the betting shows and racing results. JT, who had the most wonderful voice and could do great impressions of some of the top Shakespearean actors, was already living in Newmarket when Julie and I moved there. I was one of the first to be informed of his death. He lived with his wife, Ginny, in Doris Street. One night we got a call from Ginny, who was distraught because John had fallen over. She said she thought he was dead. Sadly she was right. I told her to dial 999, but by the time I got there John had already left us.

Happy to report, still very much with us is Graham Goode, who I knew from the beginning as we were trainee commentators at the same time. I always loved GG's delivery and Julie says he sometimes had the ability to make the hairs stand up on the back of her neck. Even I haven't been able to do that. I don't think I ever heard GG call the wrong winner. Most commentators at some point in their career do that – I know I have – but if GG did I never heard him.

In 2000 Simon Holt took over from GG as Channel 4's principal commentator and an outstanding one he is as well. Mac always calls Simon 'the languid one' and for good reason. He is so laid-back. When he sits on a chair he can't even sit up straight, he has to lean back. The only time I've ever seen Simon uptight or agitated is on the golf course. With a club in his hand he turns into a different person. One bad shot and the club gets thrown to the ground and the expletives start pouring out of his mouth. The transformation is astonishing. Whenever I've played golf with him I've found it hard to believe it's the same person I see on racecourses. But anywhere other than a golf course Simon is the loveliest guy you could meet and probably the best commentator in the business right now as well – me included!

Also lovely from top to toe is Tanya Stevenson, who has become Channel 4's main betting reporter following the axing of Mac. Even before Mac was dropped Tanya was doing far more days and deservedly so because she knows her subject inside out and has a real warmth to her that I think viewers appreciate. The viewers might even have me to thank as I was instrumental in making Tanya part of the team. Not that she wasn't part of the team before I was involved. She was, but her role was off screen. During *The Morning Line* she would sit to the side of Mac and pass him details of the market moves that were coming in, which he would then relay. The viewers would not have known that Tanya was doing this, not at least until the day I asked the cameraman to pan right and bring Tanya into shot. 'Come on Tanya,' I said. 'Tell us what's happening.'

She did and has been telling us ever since. I'm delighted for her. I've known Tanya since she was a kid, when she would stand next to her father in the betting ring, where he worked as a bookie. She would say to me: 'I bet mine beats yours.' I'd reply back that I bet it doesn't, but more often than not it did! Even then she was lovely. She was taking money off me but she was lovely. I really must have liked her!

There were so many great days and so many great moments during my time on Channel 4 that it would be impossible to fit them all in this book. People sometimes ask me, 'what was your favourite meeting?' The honest answer was always that my favourite meeting was the next one. I loved my job and as soon as I had finished the last Channel 4 programme I was looking forward to the next one.

I can, however, reveal here for the first time that something I did on *Channel 4 Racing* was partly responsible for one of the biggest events in British music over the last few decades – nothing less than the decision of Robbie Williams to quit Take That in 1995.

I became good friends with Robbie's dad Pete Conway on the celebrity golf circuit. Pete is an avid racing fan and he explained to me how he and Rob once lived in a caravan for three months on Yarmouth racecourse while Pete, like his son a tremendous singer, performed a summer season in the town. One day in 2012 Pete rang me for a natter and, aware that there was a lot of noise in the background, I asked him where he was. 'I'm on the bus,' he said. I asked him if it was the number 57 – that made me chuckle – but he said, no, it was the Take That tour bus. Then he put Robbie on the phone. I also knew Robbie a little having inter-viewed him once during the Chester May meeting in the 1990s when he was there with the other Take That boys. He asked me if I remembered that interview. I told him, of course I did, and then he said: 'You're the man that made me go solo.' That didn't really make sense to me, but then he explained that later that day the band's manager had phoned him and given him a severe dressing down for doing a TV interview without permission. Rob said to me: 'I told him to f*** off and decided that enough was enough.'

Another memorable Chester interview involved Bryan Robson while he was still captain of Manchester United. He asked me if during the day he could bring a young lad to the Channel 4 position as he wanted to give him some experience of doing live television. That's exactly what he did and it meant I got the first ever TV interview with Ryan Giggs. I was told John Motson was particularly unhappy about that! And those were not the only big interviews I did at Chester. Years later I was there for Channel 4 and interviewing Michael Owen. I looked over his shoulder and there was his Manchester United team-mate, and also one of his racing stable's owners, Wayne Rooney. I stepped across to talk to Wayne and unfortunately trod on his foot. Even more unfortunately, Wayne had just come out of hospital having undergone a leg operation. I could have finished his career.

Fortunately I didn't. Wayne is still playing football and Robbie is still wowing his fans. I'm still going as well! I'm no longer on Channel 4 but I'm definitely still going. All being well, I will be for years to come.

FIFTEEN

'IT'S ONLY A PASSING SHOWER'

Over a six-year period between 1994 and 2000 I made 129 return trips to Dubai. Every time I boarded the plane I turned left and travelled first class. While in Dubai I stayed in a special suite that was reserved for my use in a five-star hotel. I lived one life in Britain and another in Dubai because Sheikh Mohammed decided that his own part of the racing world needed a bit of the Tommo treatment.

It was perhaps the most extraordinary period of my life. I once read somewhere about David Frost's constant trips to and from America. He would present two live chat shows a week, one in Britain and one in the States. He went back and forth from one country to the next, just like Len Goodman and Bruno Tonioli have done for the last few years when working as judges on *Strictly Come Dancing* and its American equivalent show *Dancing with the Stars*. But long before Len and Bruno were holding their paddles both here and there, I was doing the same. I was a very lucky boy indeed.

It all began thanks to a conversation with Henry Cecil in the autumn of 1993. Julie and I had been for dinner at Warren Place, during which Henry had asked us if we had ever visited Dubai. At that point Henry still trained for Sheikh Mohammed bin Rashid Al Maktoum, who was then not only Crown Prince of Dubai but also Britain's most powerful racehorse owner. Henry said that he had been to Dubai a few months earlier and had found it to be a wonderful place. The sheikh was also trying to improve racing in the emirate and so Henry felt it was the sort of place I might find interesting. A few months later, early in 1994, I took up Henry's suggestion and went to Dubai for an international jockeys' challenge competition that was being staged at Nad Al Sheba racecourse. I liked what I saw but felt it could be so much better. Moreover, I thought I was the one who could make it better. So I asked Sheikh Mohammed to let me.

I sought permission to see him during a meeting at York that he was attending with members of his family and entourage. I had interviewed him a couple of times, so he knew me in a small way, and the fact that he agreed to see me hinted that he was at least prepared to listen to whatever I might have to say. Even so, I was extremely nervous as I walked into a large room that was full of what must have been 50 men. Everyone in the room stood up. 'That's nice of them,' I thought, but then it dawned on me that if Sheikh Mohammed stood up, so did everyone else. He asked me to sit next to him. I did and told him in some detail what I wanted to do.

I explained to him that I shared his vision for making Dubai a great racing nation but that to achieve the vision he first had to make Dubai a great place to go racing. At that point I did not think it was. I told him that Nad Al Sheba, the emirate's main racecourse, lacked atmosphere. What little racecourse commentary there was could not have been described as particularly impressive, and for most of a raceday there was nothing to be heard but silence. I said to him that if he let me work for him in Dubai, commentating on the racing and acting as a master of ceremonies between races, I would give Nad Al Sheba the sort of boost and feelgood factor I was adamant it needed.

'Derek,' he said. 'I must go now to watch my horse in the next race. As for what you have suggested for Dubai . . . do it."

Over the next six years I did do it. I worked at my first Nad Al Sheba meeting in the autumn of 1994 at the start of the track's new season. I did everything I had promised Sheikh Mohammed I would do. I commentated, I presented and I interviewed, all of them in my usual style. I wanted to get the paying customers more engaged with what they were watching and I think I managed that. During the early hours of the following morning I received a phone call that showed Sheikh Mohammed felt the same.

It was 2am when the hotel room phone started ringing. Julie had come out with me for the first working trip and we were staying in the old Dubai Hilton, a hotel that has since been demolished. Bleary-eyed, I picked up the phone. It was John Letts, one of Sheikh Mohammed's closest advisers. 'Tommo, it's John,' he said. 'I'll see you downstairs in ten minutes.'

'John,' I said, more than a bit confused. 'It's 2am. We're on the 7am red-eye flight back home. What's going on?'

'Never mind that,' he said. 'Just meet me down here in ten minutes.'

Julie, who had been woken by the noise, asked me what was happening. I told her I didn't really have the faintest idea, which was absolutely true.

When I got to the hotel lobby area John was there waiting as promised.

'Sorry to have got you out of bed Tommo,' he said. 'It's just that the boss wanted you to have this little present before you went home. It's a couple of gifts, one for you and one for Julie.'

Still confused, I thanked John, who left the hotel and wished me a good flight. I went back to the room and found a bolt upright Julie, who by now was wide awake and seemingly a bit expectant.

'What's that you've got, darling?' she asked me.

I didn't know so I opened the bag to find out. Inside were two boxes. One contained a very nice gentleman's watch. Inside the other was a ring. It wasn't just a ring, though. It was what looked like a very expensive ring.

It just so happened that not long before then I'd asked Julie if she would be my wife. I hadn't actually presented her with a ring but now there didn't seem much point in me buying one. Sheikh Mohammed had done it for me. Julie did not quite see it that way.

'I can't wear an expensive ring that another man has given me,' she said. 'We'll have to exchange it.'

I could sort of see where she was coming from, so when I returned to Dubai the following week Julie came with me again and we went to the shop where the ring had been bought. We explained what we wanted to do and first asked how much the ring had cost. The owner of the shop told us the price, which we translated on a calculator into sterling. The ring was worth £6,000.

Blimey.

Julie, who thought this was wonderful news, was then shown an array of rings and looked closely at a few before deciding on the one she wanted. I asked how much it would cost, expecting the replacement to be in the same price range as the one we were exchanging.

'In sterling, sir, it will be around £12,000.'

Oh dear. That was a big shock. The news disturbed me greatly. I explained to Julie that she couldn't possibly have that one.

'Derek, you are so mean,' she shouted, before bursting into tears and storming out of the shop. I ran out after her.

'I'm sorry darling, I didn't mean to upset you,' I said, which she took to mean that I was backtracking on what I said. That hadn't been what I'd meant at all, but before I could explain what I actually had meant, Julie had walked back into the shop and told the owner that I'd changed my mind and was now going to buy her the ring.

We left the shop with Julie in possession of a £12,000 ring. Sheikh Mohammed's generosity had cost me £6,000. I was devastated. It was going to take quite a few Dubai trips to claw that back.

Fortunately, I was going to be making plenty of Dubai trips over the coming months and years.

Thanks to Sheikh Mohammed, from November to March each year I lived an incredible life. On the Monday or Tuesday I would either commentate somewhere in Britain or open a betting shop, then generally on a Wednesday I would fly to Dubai from Heathrow, every time with Emirates and always in possession of a first-class ticket. The flights were always paid for by Sheikh Mohammed, as was the rather nice car that would collect me from the airport and take me straight to where I lived for most of the six years when in Dubai, the Royal Meridien beach resort and spa hotel. Pam Wilby, the general manager of the hotel, always ensured I was given suite number 607, which was magnificent, as was the rest of the hotel. For the rest of Wednesday and then from early on Thursday I would sit by the pool with a copy of the local racing newspaper, *Al Adiyat*, doing my homework and research for that evening's Nad Al Sheba meeting.

Once at the races I would work my socks off. I commentated on each race and then went back down to the paddock, passing through the royal box as I did so. In the paddock I would interview trainers, jockeys, sponsors and special guests, plus get people involved in the various tipping competitions that took the place of betting, which, of course, in Dubai is illegal. Once racing finished I would have dinner with friends and then on Friday morning I would get the early flight back to London and then head off to whichever racecourse I was needed at for *The Morning Line* on Saturday. Each year for most weeks over those five months that's how I lived, except for those weeks in which Nad Al Sheba would also race on a Sunday, in which cases I would have to get the last flight to Dubai on a Saturday night after working for Channel 4 in the afternoon. I was busy but, my word, it was some fun.

In those days I was young enough not to get tired by the constant travelling and heavy workload. The only way in which it was difficult was in the demands it made on time that should really have been spent with my family. On days when I ought to have been taking the opportunity to visit my sons Alex and James in Scotland I was in Dubai. Then later on when India was born, the trips to Dubai again meant I was not enjoying the quality family time I should have been doing, even if it was just the chance to see my baby daughter

170

before she went to bed. I knew what I was missing out on, but this seemed too good an opportunity to pass up. I had been personally hired by Sheikh Mohammed and was getting the chance to work as one of his lieutenants. I was therefore able to get to know him reasonably well and I admired both him and his family.

When I first started out Sheikh Mohammed's elder brother Sheikh Maktoum was still ruler of Dubai, which meant Sheikh Mohammed had more time to enjoy himself and indulge his passion for racing. The sport meant a lot to him – and of course still does today – and he wanted to enhance Dubai's standing in the racing world. To help him achieve that he got all the right people into Dubai. He wanted to show off Nad Al Sheba to anyone of importance who would come. On one occasion he was escorting the Aga Khan around the racecourse and was keen to show him a new stables block that had been built. After he had taken the Aga around the grandstands, the weighing room and other public facilities, he took him to the swanky stable block and started to take him inside only to be stopped by a mean-looking guard.

'You cannot come in here,' said the guard.

In Dubai nobody says that to Sheikh Mohammed. If he wants to go somewhere he goes there. His word is the last word and when he speaks you listen, so at face value this was a monumentally embarrassing moment. But seizing the moment, Sheikh Mohammed turned around to the Aga and said: 'You see. My security is so good that even I can't get in here.'

It was brilliant. He had turned a negative into a positive just through a few inspired words.

Another famous visitor one evening was the former Irish Taoiseach, Garret FitzGerald. Part of my job was to meet and greet some of the great and the good who came to Dubai, so I was dispatched to say hello to Mr FitzGerald, who was stopping off in Dubai on the way back from an international convention. I interviewed him on the racecourse and asked him to tell all the racegoers what he thought about Dubai.

'Ah, it's a fantastic place,' he said. 'I'm very fond of the family, the erm, the erm . . .' I could see he was struggling so, knowing that I was not in camera shot, I mouthed the word, 'Maktoums', and got the visiting dignitary out of a hole.

Less enjoyable was the brief time I spent in 1999 with the lady who once stayed in the Royal Meridien suite next door to my own. I discovered that the lady in question was none other than the American actress Bo Derek, who loves her racing and was in Dubai for that reason. I thought it would be a neighbourly think to do to knock on her door, introduce myself and welcome her to Dubai. I duly knocked and when the door opened a rather small lady with blonde hair answered it.

Her lack of inches somewhat took me aback, but when I regained my composure I said: 'Hi, I'm your neighbour. I thought it would be nice to say "hello".'

Old Bo didn't seem to think it was nice at all. She just looked at me stony-faced, not a glimmer of a smile on her face. There wasn't even a grunt. This was not going well. She was looking at me while I was looking at her. I had to think of something to say that might turn things around. Always able to think on my feet, I thought of something. It was a moment of genius.

'You know what, we've both got something in common,' I said.

She gave me a look but said nothing.

'We're both called Derek.'

She continued to give me a look and continued to say nothing. 'You're Bo Derek and I'm Derek Thompson.'

I chuckled. With my little joke I'd made myself laugh. That happens quite often.

I carried on looking at Bo with one of my nice friendly grins, hoping that she might at least titter at us both being Dereks. She didn't. She shut the door in my face.

I knew the meeting hadn't gone very well, so I was a little uneasy when I was asked to interview her on the racecourse. I thought I'd start with a few words to break the ice and put her at her ease.

'Well,' I said. 'Here's a girl I met a little earlier, ho, ho, ho.'

She didn't 'ho, ho, ho' back. She just gave me the same look I'd been handed outside her hotel room door.

I'm not entirely sure that she liked me. But Sheikh Mohammed did. And Sheikh Mohammed had an idea that would forever change the face of racing in Dubai and the rest of the world.

The first I heard about the Dubai World Cup was from Sheikh Mohammed himself. It was in 1995 and I was making my way down from the commentary box to ground level. Passing through the royal box on the way, which I had to do to get from one place to the other, I saw the boss sitting alone reading a pamphlet, which turned out to be a feasibility study into a race he wanted to stage at Nad Al Sheba.

'I've got an idea for a new race, a race that would attract the best horses in the world,' he said. 'I would call it the Dubai World Cup.'

I told him it sounded like a fantastic idea. He asked me what distance I thought the World Cup should be run over. I was extremely flattered to be asked and it was lovely to think that he valued my opinion. I said it would have to be a mile and a quarter. Over that distance you would attract the best milers as well as the top middle-distance horses and it would also lure in the leading American horses, who very rarely raced beyond ten furlongs.

He agreed. Then I asked how much the race would be worth. He showed me a piece of paper on which a number had been written down.

'There are a lot of noughts, aren't there?' he said.

He was right. There were. The number was US$4,000,000, which does indeed contain a lot of noughts.

He meant business. A $4 million purse made the Dubai World Cup the world's richest horserace. But although he was totally serious in his plan to stage something special in Dubai, for his brainchild race to have credibility it needed to attract a field worthy of the money that was being offered – and that meant bringing Cigar to the desert.

Cigar was America's champion, an outstanding racehorse who had won the last 13 races he had contested, including the Breeders' Cup Classic, which he had landed in late October 1995, just before Sheikh Mohammed told me of his plans. Cigar was undoubtedly the biggest equine name in the Flat racing world at the time, so if Sheikh Mohammed wanted to launch the Dubai World Cup with a bang he had to get Cigar. He got him. John Letts was dispatched to America to speak to Cigar's owners, Allen and Madeleine Paulson, who had also bred the horse and had him in training with Bill Mott. The money being put up was vast, but it was still a big ask to persuade the connections of the sport's best horse to go for a new race in a country that was strange to them. Attempting to convince the Paulsons that this was a good idea proved difficult. All the usual means of persuasion were employed, such as giving the horse and his connections free travel and luxury treatment in Dubai. That, however, was not enough. What proved the deciding factor was Sheikh Mohammed allowing Mrs Paulson to bring her dogs on the private jet that was transporting them to Dubai. Sheikh Mohammed was told that if Mrs P's dogs could come so would their horse. The dogs came and so did Cigar.

The 1973 Grand National will always remain the greatest race I have commentated on, but being able to call the very first Dubai World Cup came pretty close. Cigar followed the script and fought off his American compatriot Soul Of The Matter to win by half a length. The World Cup had enjoyed a perfect first running. Its second running was not quite so straightforward.

The problem was it rained. Rain is not usually a concern in Dubai but on Saturday 28 March 1997, it very much was.

Nobody likes to see a major sporting event ruined by a monsoon, yet that's exactly what happened on that fateful day. Shortly after lunchtime it began to spit. That, in itself, was something of a novelty, but as the afternoon progressed it began to rain ever and ever harder. The sky was menacing and grey with little hope being offered that things might get better. Nobody, however, has more hope in their body than me and I decided that we had to try to be positive. All around the racecourse racegoers were rushing from one place to another trying to avoid being soaked by a torrent of biblical proportions. Everywhere you looked there was a dripping dishdash. The paddock was under water and the track was starting to resemble a river. At this point, perhaps with excessive optimism, I went on the public address and announced: 'Don't worry. It's only a passing shower.'

Very regrettably, this shower refused to pass. The Dubai World Cup seemed to have little chance of taking place but nobody wanted to give up. It was decided that the first four races should be abandoned and then we would reassess later in the hope that conditions might improve and enable the World Cup and the preceding contest, the Dubai Duty Free, to be staged. As we got closer to the time of the Dubai Duty Free the track was plainly still not fit to cope with a field of horses so that race was called off.

Sheikh Mohammed wanted to see for himself how bad things had got. Along with other members of the organising committee, which included my then Channel 4 colleague Brough Scott, he went out to have a walk on the track. The clever man that he is, Sheikh Mohammed went out without his sandals so that when he returned he only had to wash his feet. Poor Brough went out in his shoes but returned with one of them missing after it got stuck in the Dubai swamp. Even I had to admit things were looking on the gloomy side so it was no great surprise to see Sheikh Mohammed move a finger across his throat in a sign that told the world racing was abandoned.

But it actually wasn't abandoned, only postponed. Sheikh Mohammed decided that the World Cup should be run the following Thursday, which in Britain was also the first day of the Grand National meeting at Aintree. Nad Al Sheba staff worked tirelessly around the clock to get the track back in tip-top condition. Sheikh Mohammed ensured all racing professionals, plus of course the connections of the runners, were given VIP treatment

Top: I pioneered the 'walk back' interview from the winner's enclosure to the weighing room. This time I'm with Kieren Fallon. *Bottom:* At a dinner in Newmarket with three of my best mates, (from left to right) Richard Levin, John Francome and Mark Edmondson, who just happens to be Frankel's solicitor.

Top: My final day on Channel 4 Racing: the morning production meeting on William Hill King George VI Chase day at Kempton on 26 December 2012. As ever, Andrew Franklin (far left) leads the team. *Bottom:* Every one of them a stunner. Tommo hosting the always fiercely competitive St Leger festival best-dressed lady competition.

Top: In the dressing room of Sir Tom Jones at the MGM Grand in Las Vegas. You'll note my wife Julie has chosen to stand next to Sir Tom, not her husband. Far left is Sir Tom's manager Don Archell, next to him is Don 'Hotel California' Felder, on the other side of Julie is top rally driver Steve Graham and putting an arm around me is Willie Morgan, one of very few men to wear the number seven shirt for Manchester United.
Bottom: I have the highest regard for Sir Alex Ferguson. I can't recall him ever saying no to an interview request.

Above: With the champ: interviewing Tony McCoy for BBC Radio 5 live after his 2013 Cheltenham Festival win on At Fishers Cross. *Bottom:* Conducting a big-race draw ceremony with 'The Crafty Cockney' Eric Bristow. You might not know that after listening to the classified football results Eric can recite them all within five minutes. He's good at darts as well (© Alec Russell).

Back with the Beeb: dressed to impress for 5 live at the 2013 Cheltenham Festival. The radio kit bag I had to carry weighed an absolute ton – and that was without my packed lunch.

Top: I asked Alan Carr if he had confused the Cheltenham Festival for Royal Ascot? *Bottom left:* The actor Jimmy Nesbitt, a real racing nut. *Right:* Walking down the Aintree steps with one of my greatest supporters Frankie Dettori. We were both ambassadors for the Bob Champion Cancer Trust Grand National Legends race and were proud to be so.

Top: Somewhere I don't get to spend much time – my kitchen. *Bottom left:* With Mrs Derek Thompson at our home near Newmarket. *Bottom right:* Like mother, like daughter. India is thankfully blessed with her mother's looks, not mine.

At one of the Newmarket Guineas Balls Julie organised and which raised £500,000, in the process funding a four-wheel drive ambulance for the Newmarket gallops. I had broken my wrist not long before the picture was taken. Some individuals cruelly

while they waited for the race's new date to come around. I had to return home to fulfil work commitments but I was back in Dubai for the raceday and called home an entirely fitting winner as Singspiel passed the post first for Britain with Jerry Bailey – who had ridden Cigar 12 months earlier – wearing Sheikh Mohammed's famous maroon and white silks.

The 1998 World Cup brought the race back to America as Silver Charm won for the legendary trainer Bob Baffert and the equally legendary jockey Gary Stevens. Out in Dubai for that year's race was the broadcaster Chris Lincoln, who used to present the international feed coverage of the World Cup. Chris came up to me and asked if I would like to be introduced to Silver Charm's owners, Bob and Beverly Lewis. He said they were lovely and as American as apple pie. He was right. They were the sweetest couple you could find. You could just imagine them sitting together on a swing seat on their little porch watching the world go by. Both of them were of a certain age, so it seemed such a nice story that they had found themselves with a runner in the world's richest race. I was delighted for them when Silver Charm won and they made for great interviewees in the winner's enclosure.

'We just got lucky,' they kept saying, which was clearly true. At the end of the interview I thought I had missed an obvious question by forgetting to ask what Mr Lewis had done for a living. It turned out he was still working. He looked me in the eye and said: 'I'm the biggest distributor of Budweiser in southern California.'

I thought he might have owned the local provisions store. It turned out he was a brewing magnate!

Another quite wealthy owner won in 1999 when Almutawakel scored under Richard Hills for Sheikh Hamdan, while the race stayed in the family again the following year when Dubai Millennium, the best horse Sheikh Mohammed has ever owned and the best I have ever commentated on, romped to a stunning success under Frankie Dettori. 'This is a wonder horse,' was how I described him in a commentary that went out to a worldwide audience of 1.8 billion, even more than I used to get on *The Morning Line*.

But with Dubai Millennium my time as the voice of the Dubai World Cup, and indeed the voice of Dubai racing, ended. I was faced with a choice. Sheikh Mohammed had fallen in love with Australians and one such Aussie, Les Benton, chief executive of the Emirates Racing Association, wanted to redefine my post and expand it to include the work of a media officer. A bigger job meant the need for its holder to live full time in Dubai. Simon Crisford, Godolphin's racing manager, told me that the boss had appointed Les and if Les wanted to change things he had to stand by him. I was disappointed but I understood. I couldn't give up my work for Channel 4, not to mention everything else I did at home, but more importantly I had a wife and, at that point, three children living in Britain. The flight to Dubai is a relatively short one but I still couldn't justify emigrating. I had loved working in Dubai, loved being close to Sheikh Mohammed and loved living in suite 607. All good things come to an end. This was a very good thing, but to an end it did indeed come.

Nad Al Sheba is no more. It ceased operations in 2009 with Meydan taking its place as the World Cup's host for the first time in 2010.

Sheikh Mohammed wanted to build a racecourse that was bigger and better than any other in the world. Meydan was certainly more expensive with reports suggesting that the final bill for construction came in at $1.25 billion. For that sort of cash you can expect a large grandstand. Meydan's is on a scale that beggars belief.

During my cancer treatment I spent quite a bit of time in Dubai, making the most of the sunshine and seeing some old friends. I stayed at the racecourse hotel that runs along the perimeter of the track and gives you a spectacular view from your balcony. At 4am the floodlights come on as the horses head on to the track for morning work, which for me was great as I was out there quick as a flash with my binoculars watching them. I was enormously impressed but I'm afraid that when I returned for the Thursday evening meeting I was less impressed. Put simply, there was no one at Meydan. The place felt almost empty. Most of the cavernous grandstand was closed and in the small section open to the public the atmosphere was non-existent. Nad Al Sheba, for all that it was a very large site, had a surprisingly cosy feel to it. Meydan just seemed soulless, which a gigantic racecourse with next to nobody in it will inevitably be.

After my visit I went to see Sheikh Mohammed in the desert. He was there for an endurance race but was not actually riding in it. I asked him why. 'Derek,' he said. 'I am now the world champion. I give the others a chance.'

I loved that. But I told him I did not love Meydan in its current state. It was attracting the best horses, the best trainers, the biggest owners and the greatest prize-money, yet neither Dubai's natives nor the expatriate community seemed to want to go there.

'Sir,' I said. 'Meydan needs your help. You have to do something about it.'

Sheikh Mohammed told me to see the Meydan chief executive and chairman, Saeed Al Tayer, but he was never able to see me. I think that part of the problem is Saeed is not really a racing man. He is a former powerboat world champion but I don't think they necessarily expect to get big crowds at powerboat events. Meydan should be getting big crowds but is not. I did manage to speak to Frank Gabriel, the chief executive of the Emirates Racing Authority, but he did not seem interested in what I had to say. That, I think, was a shame.

However, if Meydan is struggling, Dubai's number-two racecourse is not. I now have a contract to act as master of ceremonies at the Sheikh Ahmed-owned Jebel Ali, a beautiful all-weather racecourse whose quality of racing is not as strong as Meydan's but still manages to be more popular with racegoers. We sometimes have more than 20,000 people coming through the gates at just under £2 a person and I make sure they enjoy themselves. I attend most of the Jebel Ali fixtures, which tend to take place on Fridays, and I love going there. We have prize draws throughout the afternoon and at a recent meeting I gave away a total of 130 electrical goods. Mobile phones, iPads, televisions, microwaves, you name it, I gave it away. We even once had a few vacuum cleaners as prizes, which meant I couldn't stop myself from announcing: 'Win one of these and you'll clean up!' That made me laugh.

I've also gained a major new involvement in the Middle East by becoming the presenter of the Sheikh Mansour Global Arabian Flat Racing Festival, a contest devised by Abu Dhabi's Sheikh Mansour, who, of course, also owns Manchester City. Lara Sawaya, the lady who organises the series, was very flattering when asking me to take the job, which ferries me around the world, from Oman to Texas and Melbourne. We promote pure-bred Arabian racing and also give a platform for lady jockeys, so I think it's a worthwhile venture on many levels.

I love every job I do and I'm certainly loving this one. The desert has indeed been very kind to Tommo.

SIXTEEN

COURT 13

The worst day of my life was Friday, 20 February 1998. I was put through the sort of torment I never want to endure again. I was humiliated, shamed and embarrassed. It all happened in Court 13 of the Royal Courts of Justice in the Strand. The great sadness is I never wanted to be there in the first place.

The story has been well documented in the past. Indeed, while it was happening it was the biggest racing story in town. When Lynda Ramsden, her husband Jack and jockey Kieren Fallon took action against Mirror Group Newspapers for an allegedly libelous comment piece in *The Sporting Life* on 11 May 1995, it seemed the whole world wanted to come and watch. Sadly for me, no day attracted more interest than the one in which I appeared for the defence. I was, as everyone by now knows, an extremely reluctant witness.

There is little need all these years later to go over the details in the minutiae. The bare structure of the story is simple. On

18 April 1995, Top Cees, trained by Lynda Ramsden, whose husband was one of the most respected punters in the business, finished fifth as 5-1 favourite in the Swaffham Handicap, a one-mile-six-furlong race staged during Newmarket's Craven meeting.

Next time out on 10 May 1995, Top Cees was a five-length winner of the Chester Cup, once again ridden by Fallon. On 11 May 1995, *The Sporting Life* published an editorial opinion piece, penned by Alastair Down, in which it claimed that when contesting the Swaffham, Top Cees had been 'not off' and that the trainer and jockey had been guilty of cheating.

In none of the above did I have any direct involvement and yet I ended up being a central figure in the trial that took place nearly three years later.

There is no little irony in the fact that only a few years after that controversial Newmarket race, Channel 4 axed its annual coverage of the Craven meeting. How I wish Channel 4 had done so before 1995. If it had, I would not have been forced – for forced is what I was – to go through the misery that took place in Court 13.

My time in the witness box stemmed from a conversation I had with Kieren in the Old Plough pub in Ashley, where I was having dinner on the night of the Swaffham Handicap. For legal reasons I am unable to repeat what I told the court was said in that conversation, but on the morning after my evening in the Old Plough I was back at Newmarket racecourse for the next day of the Craven meeting. During the production meeting I mentioned having spoken with Kieren. I clearly did not do that through a desire to bring up the conversation in that afternoon's programme, but I did agree to arrange an interview with Kieren. That should have been the end of it for me, but when the libel action was taken against Mirror Group Newspapers, I was subpoenaed to appear as a defence witness. Alastair, as well as a senior writer for *The Sporting Life*, was also a relatively new member of the Channel 4 team, thus providing a link between what I said in the production meeting and the demand that I appear on behalf of Mirror Group Newspapers at the trial.

Through my solicitor, Razi Mireskandari, I did everything I possibly could to avoid giving evidence. I attempted to exploit all conceivable legal loopholes, but when the subpoena was served on me I had no choice. I did not want to be there. I knew by appearing in court I would be damaging my relationship not only with Kieren but potentially with others in racing, who might no longer feel able to speak to me privately or even publicly. I was aware that a prosecution barrister would attempt to discredit me. It was wholly obvious to me that by going to court I was in an absolutely no-win position. But I had no choice. I had to go.

The days leading up to my appearance were desperate. I was spending a lot of time in Dubai while working at Nad Al Sheba, but at home Julie had not long ago given birth to our first child together, our daughter India. It was already a stressful and hectic time for that reason alone. We needed this extra pressure like a hole in the head and the pressure seemed to intensify all the time. It was horrible in the extreme.

Had I not responded positively to the subpoena I would have been in danger of being sent to jail myself. Julie agreed there was nothing else to do, but she went into the case telling me she hoped the jury would not believe my evidence. That might sound like a strange thing to say, but she felt for the long-term sake of my career it would be better for me if I was not seen to be the one bringing down the career of one of the sport's highest-profile riders. Racing can be a very closed shop – as I quickly found out – and Julie felt there would be many people in racing, and even within our home town of Newmarket, who would turn against me after I gave my evidence.

On the dreaded day I went to London without Julie as she needed to stay at home with India. I travelled by train and then taxi to The Strand and then, for the first time in my life, was shown into a court room. I had never once stepped foot in such a place. The closest I had come was when watching programmes like *Rumpole of the Bailey* and *Perry Mason* on television. It was an alien place to me and a terrifying place as well. I knew what was coming.

My nerves were so bad I could barely read out the words that were in front of me. In my line of sight were the Ramsdens, Jack and Lynda. They had never been great friends, but we had been out to dinner in the past and I thought I knew them well enough.

Their eyes bore into me like daggers. I could see their barrister, Patrick Milmo, waiting for his turn to tear into me, like a lion stalking its prey. First up, though, was the other side.

One of the opening things Richard Hartley, the defence QC, said in his questioning of me was that I had been 'compelled to give evidence', to which I wholeheartedly agreed. 'I gain nothing out of this," I said. 'Believe you and me, it's the worst feeling in the world sitting here.'

I spoke in hushed tones. David Ashforth, who was reporting on the case for *The Sporting Life*, described me in his article the following day as 'hangdog, shoulders bowed, head bowed, frowning, in almost constant state of open-mouthed surprise'. That pretty much sums it up. I couldn't believe any of it was happening. Just getting through the questions put to me by Hartley was bad enough. The Milmo massacre was much, much worse.

He accused me of telling 'an outrageous lie' about Kieren. He ripped to shreds my reputation as a telephone tipster and sought to challenge my professional credentials, just as he had done when Channel 4's Jim McGrath had appeared in court earlier in the trial. I have to pay due credit to Milmo.

It pains me to say it, but he was outstanding and, in my opinion, far superior to his opposite number. It seemed to me I was being treated as though I was the accused party. I was being discredited. I told the court that I was being put through 'public humiliation' and that what was taking place made this undoubtedly 'the worst day of life'. And it was the worst. By far the worst.

One of my most abiding memories of the whole traumatic experience is being at home that night, getting in a hot bath, putting a wet flannel over my face and crying. I have never felt so awful. I had been personally destroyed in the name of British justice.

Five days after my evidence was given the case ended in defeat for Mirror Group Newspapers. The Ramsdens and Kieren had been successful in their libel claim. There was, however, a little victory of sorts for the newspaper in the compensation that came with the verdicts.

In his closing words the judge had said if the jury found in favour of the Ramsdens and Fallon, they should be advised that damages of £50,000 each would be 'niggardly', while £125,000 would be deemed 'extravagant'. Lynda Ramsden received £75,000 and Kieren £70,000, but Jack Ramsden was awarded the 'niggardly' sum of £50,000. Nevertheless, Mr Ramsden still felt able to stand on the steps of the Royal Courts and describe my actions as 'utterly contemptible'. He said that he had viewed my presence in court – my enforced presence – as tantamount to blackmail and a threat. That, of course, was complete nonsense. In fact it was an utterly contemptible thing to say.

But at least it was over. Or it was in part. I still had to see how I would be received in the racing world. On that front there was, I'm pleased to say, much more good news than bad. Andrew Franklin, my outstanding boss at Channel 4 Racing, rang me and said that I would have a job for as long as I wanted one. Andrew being Andrew, that was to be expected. However, others offered support that might not have been so expected. I received lovely letters from the top Irish trainer Dermot Weld and from Ben Hanbury, a former Classic-winning trainer based in Newmarket. Pat Eddery, then still a leading rider and a very high-profile and successful colleague of Kieren's, gave me his backing and so did Michael Hills, one of my best mates among the jockeys. Sadly, a few good friends were not there for me when I needed them.

A few days after the trial ended I was back working in Dubai. Whenever I was at Nad Al Sheba I always went into the jockeys' room before racing. I did so again. After I entered the room it went quiet. I sensed I was in trouble.

After the first race the winning jockey declined my request for an interview. I was definitely in trouble. I thought that maybe I had misinterpreted the weighing room's reaction earlier on, so I asked a rider who was also a very good friend if he would come out and help me fill five minutes of airtime. He turned me down.

I have never forgotten that. I am far more inclined to forgive someone than Julie, who reckons that my willingness to let bygones be bygones is actually a character flaw on my part, but whilst I might forgive, I can't always forget. And I haven't forgotten that particular individual turning his back on me in my hour of need.

But then I was rescued from an unexpected source.

'I'll come out for an interview Tommo.'

It was Frankie Dettori.

There was no bigger name in racing and there still isn't. He willingly put his neck on the line for me and I have always remembered that.

I have an awful lot of time for Frankie. When he first came over to Britain from Italy he was once a touch ignorant in one of our first meetings. He must have known he had behaved badly because he then sent to the house what appeared to be the entire contents of the local florists. Many years later, he was a good friend through my cancer struggle. Frankie recently went through a tough time of his own but he is more than strong enough, and undoubtedly more than talented enough, to get back to the top.

Having Frankie on side was a huge help, as once he nodded his head in approval most of his fellow riders followed like sheep.

That entitled me to continue my broadcasting career as before, and that has included regularly interviewing Kieren. I have no problem with Kieren. I do, however, have a problem with the Ramsdens, although not with their daughter Emma. After the Top Cees trial I worked with her on numerous occasions for Channel 4 and I don't believe there were ever any difficulties. She is a lovely girl and we get on great. In fact, I discovered that if you throw her a sweet from four feet away she can catch it in her mouth. You have to be impressed with anyone who can do that.

The pain of the trial and my court appearance will never fully go away but thankfully it is now in the increasingly distant past. There is, however, one postscript that is worth mentioning. Less than a month after the trial ended Top Cees went to the Cheltenham Festival and won one of the meeting's showpiece handicap hurdles, the Coral Cup.

I had always liked the horse and so was pleased for him, but as he returned to the sport's most hallowed winner's enclosure a ripple of booing could clearly be heard as could the sound of people chanting, 'Tommo, Tommo, Tommo'.

It seemed to me that the racing public was making a point. That, I thought, was very nice indeed.

SEVENTEEN

CHANNEL 4: PART TWO

For how long does a thank you last? Is there a length of time over which gratitude should be shown for a good deed done? I can't give you an answer to either question. You might be better off asking Channel 4.

Without me, *Channel 4 Racing* might no longer exist. That sounds a tad conceited but it's true. If you don't believe me, ask Andrew Franklin, the man who produced *Channel 4 Racing* throughout my nearly three decades on the programme. He will tell you the same thing and has made very clear to me I should tell you as well. I was, in rather a big way, the saviour of *Channel 4 Racing*, but I didn't do the saving until 2007. My position within the team had taken a slight knock six years before then.

Brough Scott chose to resign his position as Channel 4's lead racing presenter in 2001. Brough had been the face of *Channel 4 Racing* ever since the network took over ITV's midweek racing coverage in 1984. Before then he had been ITV's main racing presenter. He was as much an integral part of racing on television as Sir Peter O'Sullevan but he had decided it was time to bow out. I was surprised. Until Brough told me his news I had no inkling about what he was going to do and when he did tell me I told him he was making the wrong decision. Brough is the Peter Pan of racing but even though he looks much younger than his years, he certainly isn't ancient and he definitely wasn't in 2001. But Brough had good timing as a jockey and equally good timing as a broadcaster. He was adamant it was right for a younger man to take up the principal job. I was a younger man and I was also Brough's number two. Not surprisingly I wanted to be the new number one.

I thought I had a decent chance of being picked. More importantly, I thought I deserved to be picked. Among the *Channel 4 Racing* team at the time I was jointly the most senior member of the team along with Jim McGrath, but Jim was our top paddock pundit and carried out that role much more often than he presented. John Francome was probably the most popular member of the team but, like Jim, he specialised in punditry. When Brough was not presenting on a Saturday or at a midweek meeting I was invariably the one who stood in for him. I like to think I was the safest pair of hands we had and I believed I merited a crack at taking on responsibility for leading our biggest days. I still believe I merited that chance but the chance came not to me but to another.

It was Andrew who phoned me with the news.

'Derek, we're going with Alastair Down,' he said.

I was astonished. I had clearly had issues with Alastair in the past due to the Top Cees trial, but I'd like to think my surprise was not due to personal resentment. Indeed, although I probably wouldn't call Alastair a great mate, and I'm sure he feels the same about me, I continued to get on perfectly well with him. I considered him to be a good guy and I respected him hugely as a writer.

I also respected him as a broadcaster, but he had been working on television for far less time than me and, put simply, I thought I was the better man for the job.

Andrew was kind and understood my disappointment. His reasoning for the decision was also flattering. He said that it was felt Channel 4 couldn't afford to lose me as me. He said they needed Tommo and if I was promoted to become the lead anchor I couldn't continue doing all the things that Tommo did. I was the only person on the Channel 4 team who could pretty much do anything. I could present, I could commentate, I could work as a pundit and I could interview anyone I was asked to interview. Andrew explained that I was invaluable to Channel 4 doing what I already did and if I was given Brough's job they wouldn't really be able to replace me.

Perhaps he was right. I also have to admit that my disappointment did not last long. For about a week I was absolutely gutted but that feeling really did only last for a week. Even Julie says that I've always been something of the clown on Channel 4. I don't mind that description at all. If I was the clown, I was a clown who could also be serious, but maybe a clown was not the right fit for the top job. As is my way, I put the disappointment to the back of my mind, locked away any sadness in a mental box, and told myself that I still had a great job with Channel 4 and that I should think myself lucky. To be fair to Alastair, he even had the decency to come to our house in Newmarket and offer Julie and myself what was in some ways an apology. Given what had just happened, and what had happened only a little while earlier in court, that was a generous act and it was appreciated.

'I'm sorry Derek,' he said. 'You must think I'm your nemesis.'

Then Julie, as quick as a flash, said: 'Don't tell him you're his nemesis Alastair. He'll think you're talking about a bloody ride at Alton Towers.'

Which, to be fair, it is.

So Alastair got the job. I carried on doing what I had been doing before, the only difference being I was doing it under the on-air leadership of Alastair as opposed to Brough. In a sense nothing really changed. I carried on as the main presenter of *The Morning Line* and I appeared as part of the Channel 4 squad at most of the principal meetings, stepping in to replace Alastair when he was not available.

One thing that did start to change, however, was Channel 4's attitude to racing. Editorially, we seemed to be as committed as ever, but financially less so. It seemed increasingly the case that Channel 4's bosses were no longer prepared to stump up the money that was needed to cover the sport properly. Racing is not cheap to do well on television. If you are producing snooker, bowls, or even tennis or cricket, it's much more straightforward, mainly because the physical site you need to bring to the screen is so much smaller. Less cameras are required which means less money is spent. Racecourses tend to be pretty big places and you cannot do it with a single camera. Just rigging up a race-course with all the necessary technical equipment is at least a day's work. If you want to do racing properly you can't do it on the cheap, but that's what from time to time we were being asked to do. The budget Andrew and Highflyer had to work with got progressively more difficult. Times were starting to get hard.

They got even harder when Channel 4 started to play poker with the sport. Certain demands were made, the main one being that a financial subsidy would have to be paid for Channel 4 to continue its long association with racing. The Levy Board was asked to provide racecourses with money that in turn was passed on to Channel 4 in the form of a production support payment. Towards the end of 2006 Channel 4 upped the ante and insisted it would need racing to secure a programme sponsor for it to continue. The Tote, under its totesport wing, stepped in, which was a relief, but there was understandably a raising of eyebrows at the BBC. The Beeb, which itself was starting to scale back on how much racing it covered, paid a significant rights fee to televise racing. Channel 4, its racing rival, was effectively now being paid to cover the sport. One scenario did not seem to fit comfortably with the other, especially as Channel 4 was also warning racing that it would walk away from its commitment to the sport if the rights to the Cheltenham Festival were given back to the BBC.

In the summer of 2007 crisis point was reached. The Tote had decided to end its backing of the programme after only one year of a three-year deal. Channel 4 did not hesitate in its reaction. Andrew Thompson, the channel's head of sport, let it be known, both publicly and privately, that unless a new sponsor could be found, coverage of racing would end. This was desperate news. What Channel 4 provided was a shop window. On every single Saturday we broadcast at least two hours of live racing on top of a one-hour magazine show in the morning. If Channel 4 carried out its threat to say goodbye, the BBC would have taken the Cheltenham Festival and some of Channel 4's most important Flat days, but the vast majority of the terrestrial exposure Channel 4 provided would have disappeared.

By the time we got to York's Ebor meeting that August racing was extremely anxious. Those of us who worked for *Channel 4 Racing* felt the same. The betting exchange Betfair and the bookmaker Bet365 were both spoken of as potential replacements for the Tote, but nothing happened. No deal was signed, no progress made. There was a genuine feeling within the Channel 4 camp that we were doomed. That was certainly the assessment made by Andrew Franklin when he addressed the team at the start of one of the York production meetings. The expectation, we were informed, was that if no progress was made by the end of the week, Channel 4 would announce that it was regrettably ending its racing coverage at the end of the year. When he told us all how grim things had become I started to think. I believed I might just have a possible solution.

'Has anybody spoken to Sheikh Mohammed about this?' I asked.

Andrew said that he couldn't be sure but his belief was nobody had. I thought it was about time somebody did.

'Could I be excused for the rest of the meeting please, boss?' I asked. I explained that I wanted to make a phone call that I believed could save *Channel 4 Racing*. Andrew readily agreed and I left the meeting.

I rang Sheikh Mohammed's office. Thanks to our work together in Dubai I knew him probably better than anyone else in the media apart from Brough, who had encouraged him to start the *Racing Post* just over 20 years earlier. His Highness had done that because Brough explained it would be very much for the good of racing. So would saving Channel 4's racing coverage. Sheikh Mohammed was in Dubai when I spoke to his aide. I told him that *Channel 4 Racing* was going to fold unless a sponsor could be found and asked him whether the boss might be interested in coming to the rescue. In total our conversation probably lasted for less than a minute. The aide just said, 'leave it with me', and that was that.

Within half an hour I had a phone call from Ahmed Al Shaikh, the managing director of Dubai Media Incorporated.

'What's happening, Derek?' he asked. 'I've been told to go to the airport, fly to London and do a deal to sponsor *Channel 4 Racing*. Please tell me what's going on.'

I explained to Ahmed what I knew. I had been told Channel 4 was demanding a total of £4 million, equivalent to £2m for each of the two years, 2008 and 2009, that were left on its existing contract to broadcast 80 days of racing a year. Ahmed took in all the necessary information and after landing in London set about starting talks with Channel 4. Ahmed, who was Sheikh Mohammed's main TV man, was acting for Dubai Holding, which owned Dubai's seven-star Burj Al Arab hotel and had international interests including the Travelodge hotel chain and the Tussauds group. Dubai Holding belongs to the Dubai government but is controlled by Sheikh Mohammed, so essentially he was the one who was offering to sponsor *Channel 4 Racing*. The talks took a while to be completed but in September 2007 a £4m sponsorship deal was announced under which *Channel 4 Racing* would continue and Dubai would be given mini-advertisements at the start and end of every *Channel 4 Racing* programme plus slots into and out of all the commercial breaks.

We were saved. When the deal was announced I was thanked by my Channel 4 team-mates but not by the Channel 4 high command. I'm sure they must have known what I had done, but they didn't say anything. For me, that might have been an unwelcome sign of things to come.

The two remaining years of the Channel 4 rights deal came and went. Channel 4 retained its contract for a further three years from 2010 to 2012, once again fending off the BBC's attempt to regain the Cheltenham Festival and a handful of Newmarket's showpiece Flat days. To be fair to the BBC, it did not push hard as it did not want Channel 4 to pull out of racing, which Channel 4 had once again clearly intimated would be the outcome if its crown jewels were handed to the corporation.

There were, however, differences in how we did things from the start of 2010. Money was even tighter. Highflyer had faced a very stiff challenge from the BBC's racing producer Sunset+Vine for the Channel 4 production contract. Highflyer won but gossip on the street was that Sunset+Vine had come very close to nicking the gig, which would have put it in the unusual and strange position of having responsibility for both the BBC's and Channel 4's racing coverage at the same time. Although successful, Highflyer was told it had to rein in spending even more than it already had. Channel 4 wanted to save £800,000 a year, which meant an average of £10,000 had to be knocked off every programme. Inevitably, our wages were cut, which was clearly bad news for me. It was not, however, the only bad news.

I had only just returned home from a short stay in hospital when I noticed a voicemail message from Channel 4's head of sport Andrew Thompson. I rang him back and after a few pleasantries were exchanged he came out with the reason for his original call. I was told Channel 4 was going to change the way in which its racing coverage was fronted. In future there was going to be a clear division between what it did on the Flat and over jumps. Each code would have a presentation double act fronting the coverage. The double acts would be made up of four different people. I was not one of the four. I was told Alastair and Alice Plunkett had been selected to be the faces of the jumps season and that Mike Cattermole and Emma Spencer were taking over on the Flat. I knew immediately that this development was bad news for me and Andrew Thompson clearly realised how I was feeling. He attempted to sweeten the pill. He said Channel 4 wanted to increase the importance shown to the second-site meeting and, to that end, wanted to appoint a presenter to host all those number-two fixtures. I was the man it wanted to appoint.

I asked if he was sure this was what he wanted to do and asked if this meant we would now have a presenting presence at all the secondary fixtures. I was told that at the vast majority we would. This at least meant I would have a steady supply of work coming from Channel 4 but it also meant I would have very few opportunities to present *The Morning Line*. That had to be based at the day's principal meeting and I was not going to be appearing at them. Nick Luck would take over in *The Morning Line* chair, leaving me to occasionally provide inserts into the programme from whichever track I was at.

It was a little like rewinding the clock a quarter of a century. From 1981 to 1985 I had been doing on *World of Sport* what Channel 4 was asking me to do now. In no way was it a positive career move but at least I would still be on Channel 4 and I also had an assurance that I would continue to have a place during the Cheltenham Festival and our other highest-profile fixtures.

The verbal promises were made but regrettably they were not kept. Prior to 2010 I had been working for Channel 4 on probably three out of every four Saturdays. In no time at all, that number dwindled to two out of every four and sometimes to only one. I went back to Andrew Thompson, who simply said that funds were even tighter than they had expected and that they could not justify having a presence at as many second-site meetings as they had hoped. I could understand that there wasn't too much money in the Channel 4 pot, but I couldn't understand why they could not find something for one of their longest-serving, most effective and popular presenters to do. It felt as though I was being ostracised by my own employer. As if to rub salt in the wound, Channel 4 gave *The Morning Line* a revamp early in 2011. I did not have a part to play. Not long after the revamp was completed Andrew Thompson left Channel 4. I was not sorry to see him go.

In his place came Jamie Aitchison, a former producer for Sunset+Vine of Channel 5's football shows. It turned out that for me Aitchison was even less of an ally than Thompson had been.

The final chapter in my career on Channel 4 began on the Saturday before the 2012 Cheltenham Festival. The *Racing Post* ran a front-page story in which it claimed that Channel 4 was set to be handed all terrestrial rights to British racing from the start of 2013. If the story turned out to be true it would have represented the crowning moment in Channel 4's racing life. It would mean we would take over the Grand National and Royal Ascot from the

BBC and additionally regain the Derby. That Saturday I was once again absent from the Channel 4 roster but I was on the team the following week at Cheltenham, by which point there seemed to be a growing feeling that it was a case of when the announcement was going to be made, not if. There was enormous excitement in the camp as we began to consider what next year was going to bring, and that excitement only heightened the following Monday when it was confirmed that Channel 4 would be the sport's sole terrestrial broadcaster for four years from 2013 to 2016.

With that announcement came another. Channel 4 was putting out to tender the contract to produce its racing coverage. Over the coming days it became evident that this was going to be anything but an easy race to win. Sunset+Vine was once again taking on Highflyer, as were At The Races (another of my employers) in a joint bid with SIS, North One Television, who had successfully produced ITV's Formula One coverage, and IMG, the biggest sports production company in the business but a company lacking any sort of history in horseracing.

What had been an exciting time very quickly became a nervous time. Those who worked on *Channel 4 Racing* were not employed directly by Channel 4 but by Highflyer. If Highflyer lost the contract we would lose our jobs unless Channel 4 and the new production company chose to take us on. Yet I thought Highflyer had to be the favourite. It was thanks to the work that Highflyer had done – award-winning work as well – that Channel 4 had beaten the BBC to the best events in British racing. Surely that had to put us in pole position?

Whispers on racecourses suggested such an opinion was not universally held. Sunset+Vine was named as the one to beat by a lot of people, while IMG boss Graham Fry was making public comments that underlined how seriously the company was taking its bid. That became very apparent when IMG poached two of Highflyer's senior production staff. Denise Large, the main director of *Channel 4 Racing*, and Sophie Veats, producer of *The Morning Line*, were asked if they would join forces with IMG if IMG won. They agreed and, as such, their names were used on the IMG bid document, along with that of former BBC racing editor Carl Hicks, although none of us knew at the time he was involved. When Denise and Sophie told Andrew Franklin and John Fairley what they had done there was a feeling that an act of great disloyalty had been committed.

What IMG lacked was people with significant racing experience. To improve its chances – and therefore to reduce Highflyer's chances – it needed to be able to promise big names on its team. By agreeing to be such names, Denise and Sophie were inevitably harming the prospects of Highflyer. Given that both had worked for Highflyer for so long, and given how many chances Andrew and John had given them, we all felt tremendously let down. There was no way Andrew and John could allow them to continue working for Highflyer, so they were taken off the team immediately. From that point on they were IMG people. Andrew and John must have known that all the knowledge and experience Denise and Sophie had gained working for Highflyer could now be used by IMG, but there was nothing that could be done about that. Personally, I hold no animosity to either Denise or Sophie, both of whom were presumably given a very good financial incentive to side with IMG. I had an enjoyable lunch with them at the Burghley Horse Trials and both assured me they had not behaved in an unscrupulous or unprofessional way. I like to see the good in people, so I believed them, but I was still stunned by how they had treated Highflyer.

By then we all knew that Denise and Sophie had backed the right horse. Just after the London Olympics had finished Channel 4 announced that IMG had won the contract to produce its racing output for the following four years and, in addition, it made public that Clare Balding would become the new lead presenter of *Channel 4 Racing*. It was devastating news. I felt sorry for myself but more sorry for Andrew Franklin and John Fairley, whose success had been Channel 4's success. They were left having to produce almost half a year of coverage knowing somebody else would soon be taking over. None of us knew if we would have a job the following year. The only presenter who knew for sure was Clare Balding – and she was still working for the BBC.

Just before Julie and I took the kids on holiday to Cornwall in late summer I got a phone call from Jamie Aitchison. Quite why he rang I don't know because he had nothing to tell me. I was feeling really rough due to the cancer treatment I was undergoing at the time. I certainly did not need this uncertainty over Channel 4, but Jamie was able to offer not a shred in the way of reassurance. I asked him if I would still have a job in January. His answer was that he wouldn't be able to let me know until the end of October or early November. He was true to his word. That was the last time he contacted me for more than three months. We were all left dangling.

In the end it became pretty horrible, for which I blame Channel 4. At Ascot on British Champions Day in late October it was obvious that those who would be working for the new-look Channel 4 team had already been offered jobs. Those of us who were not being offered jobs were not afforded the same luxury, or indeed courtesy. We knew our fate before the public announcement was made, which I think was unforgivable. John McCririck and I had worked for Channel 4 since it began covering racing in 1984. We were left to find out that we would no longer be working for the channel some days after it was public knowledge, confirmation coming in what we considered to be curt, crass and uncaring phone calls from Jamie Aitchison. What was said to us was basically that there was nothing we could do about this. We were told they had checked our contracts and that as we were only employed on freelance terms we had no means of challenging the decision. I wasn't even asked how my cancer treatment was going.

It was galling in the extreme. I was being axed, along with Mac, Mike Cattermole, Lesley Graham, Alastair Down and Stewart Machin. John Francome, to his credit, told Channel 4 what they could do with their job and declined all overtures. Once again he showed his class. After 28 years of service I was being dropped without any sort of meaningful thank you or good luck for the future. Just as hard to take was the fact that coming in our place was essentially a team dominated by the BBC personnel that Highflyer's Channel 4 team had beaten. Carl Hicks, Clare Balding, Mick Fitzgerald and Rishi Persad were all BBC people and yet all of them were given prominent roles on the Channel 4 team that would be covering the showpiece meetings that we had helped Channel 4 to capture. We beat the BBC hands down and yet *Channel 4 Racing* now seems like it is being controlled by the BBC. I felt like I had won the Champions League final only to be sacked by the manager at the blowing of the final whistle. Worse still, I had to then watch the players on the losing team go up to collect the trophy.

After almost half a lifetime of service to Channel 4, it wasn't a very nice way for our time together to end.

It's hard for me now to comment on the relaunched *Channel 4 Racing* coverage without what I say sounding like sour grapes. That's not what I want. If I say I'm not massively impressed by the new programmes, I'm saying it not through bitterness but from the perspective of someone who has years of experience in television and the broadcast media. I'd like to think I have a pretty good idea of what the *Channel 4 Racing* audience wants and I don't think that is what the audience is getting.

Both the official ratings and the polls that have been done on viewers' opinions suggest I'm right. On the Channel 4 website, the comments being posted were so negative that the page on which they were being made was removed. That speaks volumes.

I'm pleased that many of the people you never saw on screen have been retained. When I spoke to Denise and Sophie at Burghley I made a point of asking them first and foremost to keep on all the riggers. For presenters like myself there would always be some work even if Channel 4 did not want us. For some on the team there would not be as many opportunities if Channel 4 and IMG looked elsewhere. These guys and girls were the backbone of *Channel 4 Racing* and it's greatly to the benefit of *Channel 4 Racing* that they are still on the show. In terms of the on screen personnel I'm not so convinced that the right team is in place and I'm also not sure the way they are showcasing the sport is the right way. The most common criticism seems to be that the programmes just aren't fun anymore. I think that is right. For years Julie and I knew of people who had very little interest in racing but who watched and enjoyed *The Morning Line* nonetheless. Those people have switched off. Everything just seems too serious, a problem that isn't helped by having so much of the content presented from inside a studio. That's a bad idea. If you're broadcasting from a racecourse why coop yourself up in a sterile studio environment. When I worked on *World of Sport* that was one aspect of the show I found the most frustrating. It seems odd to me that Channel 4 are going back to what ITV did in the early 1980s. As a sports broadcaster you have so much more freedom and flexibility if you are outside. If there was a problem with someone's microphone Andrew Franklin could always quickly link to me and I could get him out of a hole. With a microphone in my hand I could go anywhere and talk to anyone. I would even try to interview a blade of grass if I thought it would make decent television.

The numbers suggest some people would rather watch a blade of grass being interviewed than what they're watching now. Channel 4 will talk with confidence but those in the plush London offices must be worried – and so should those in power in racing. It was a dangerous move selling everything to Channel 4. For all that I thought we were better than the BBC, I would still have continued with two channels covering racing. The BBC is the natural home for the Grand National and the BBC should still be doing it. By putting all their eggs in one basket and placing all their faith in Channel 4, racing's leaders have removed competition from the market and the value of that market will go down all the time that the number of people watching *Channel 4 Racing* continues to fall.

Races like the Grand National, the Derby, the Cheltenham Festival and Royal Ascot will always have a home on terrestrial television, but it would not surprise me if the decision to give Channel 4 this four-year contract ironically marks the beginning of the end for the weekly Saturday terrestrial coverage that has been the norm for so long. I hope I'm wrong, and I hope that *Channel 4 Racing* gets back on track, but I fear we could be in for worrying times.

My prediction is that at the end of 2016 we might find that Sky comes in to become the sport's new main partner. If they do, I'll make sure they know that Tommo is available.

EIGHTEEN

WORKING MY WAY THROUGH CANCER

I am an eternal optimist. My glass is always half full, every negative is turned into a positive and when I see a door close in front of me I look for another one to open. That is how I have always been and I guess it's how I always will be. It is an approach that has stood me in good stead and helped me to get through the occasional tough time. Having cancer was one of those times.

Cancer rather came out of the blue. I don't suppose many people expect to get it and I certainly did not. Essentially I have been a pretty healthy person. There has been the odd unfortunate incident, such as setting fire to myself as a young boy and ending up in hospital for 100 days, and the occasion in 2007 when I slipped on ice and ended up fracturing my wrist, causing more than one cruel so and so to claim I had tripped over my wallet. There was also the time the same year when I managed to get a darning needle stuck in my foot at the start of what was supposed to be a busy working day. Julie had organised for a new quilt cover to be made and one of the needles that had been used to make it fell on the floor. I trod on it. The needle went in so deep that Julie couldn't see it when she looked at the foot. Fortunately I still managed to drive from Newmarket to Sedgefield, where I was booked for a commentary shift that I clearly did not want to give up. The darning needle came along for the journey but I'm pleased to say that having gone with me to a couple of meetings, and caused considerable nausea as well, it was removed. I haven't done as much darning since but I'm also of the firm opinion that there's no point throwing away a perfectly good sock just because of a hole.

Accidents apart, I have largely managed to avoid ill health, but that changed quite dramatically in November 2009. I had been working at Doncaster on the final day of the Flat season. By the time I got home I had a really throbbing headache. Normally nothing would stop me from watching the Breeders' Cup but that night I just couldn't manage it because the pain in my head was unbearable. I went to bed early, telling Julie I reckoned I just needed an early night. I was wrong. I woke up at about 3am feeling absolutely dreadful. I was convinced something was seriously amiss. My chest felt all wrong, I could hardly breathe and I was sweating like a pig. Julie dialled 999, an ambulance came and I was rushed to hospital. When we got to Addenbrooke's they put me in a special ward for people who had contracted rare diseases. If you had been to Timbuktu and picked up typhoid this was where you went. But I hadn't been to Timbuktu. I'd only been to Doncaster.

They blasted me with everything they had but even morphine did not initially help the pain. Eventually I returned to an even keel and every possible sort of test was carried out. At first the doctors thought I had meningitis. That was bad. Even worse was

212

the realisation that I was going to have to give up my commentary shift at Wolverhampton on the following Monday. That was my first unscheduled day off in 25 years. Not surprisingly, I was very distressed, even more so when the doctors told me I didn't have meningitis and that my sudden downturn might have been due to working too hard. There and then I vowed to cut back on what I had been doing. I did, and for a whole fortnight as well.

For the two and a half years that followed I was back in tip-top condition. My 60th birthday came and went with me having no desire to slow down. The head showed signs of ageing only in the sense that I increasingly had to do more homework to keep the brain firing on all cylinders. The body was as magnificent as ever and answered my every call, until, that is, a couple of signals had me worrying that not everything was as it should have been.

For a start there was my poo. Everybody knows how their own body reacts and what they produce when they go to the toilet. After years of consistency there began to be a change in what I was doing. There was a redness in my stools that could only have been blood. It went from being now and again to again and again. More than half a lifetime earlier I had suffered with haemorrhoids but deep down I knew that this was not a case of the old Farmer Giles making an unwelcome return.

Having said that, had it been just the poo I might have been able to convince myself that the haemorrhoids had come back, but there was more than one symptom of there being a bigger problem. For years I had gone out jogging every morning. There's a field with a large hill near our house that I had long used for a brisk morning workout. I became a convert to interval training, the method brought to Britain by the legend that is Martin Pipe, a great trainer and a great guy. Martin's horses were given sharp blowouts up a hill and it seemed to work for them. My thinking was if it was good enough for Martin and Paul Nichols it was good enough for Tommo, so I did the same. I would walk down the hill and then run up it as fast and hard as I could. I would do this seven or eight times each session and it worked for me not only physically but also mentally, as while I was walking I would run through in my head what I had to do that day. The workout brought clarity to my thoughts, but through the spring of 2012 there was increasingly more confusion than clarity. I started to struggle to do up the hill what I had been able to do in the past. The deterioration in my performance was too marked and too rapid to have been linked solely to ageing. 'This is strange,' I thought. It was sufficiently strange for me to consult my doctor.

We are lucky to have a smashing local doctor, Simon Arthur, who was adamant I should undergo a colonoscopy. If you've had one of those you'll know that it is not a particularly pleasant experience, but needs must, so I went and had one. They had a feel around and when the doctor came out I was told there was definitely something up there. A week later, on the opening afternoon of Royal Ascot, I sat with Julie in the Addenbrooke's Hospital office of colorectal surgeon Richard Miller, who gave me the news. I had cancer.

Do not for a second think I was glad to be told I had a potentially fatal disease. I wasn't, but at least I knew what I was facing. The way I saw things, it would have been worse had Richard told me that they had been unable to find anything wrong. In those circumstances I would have known that something was not right but fretted over the fact that neither I nor the doctors knew what it was. But they did know and Richard told me they could do something about it. Unfortunately for me, he wanted to do that something the very next day. That wasn't practical. There were still four days of Royal Ascot to come. The meeting gives me one of my best earning opportunities of the year. With my Channel 4 job at that point hanging in the balance, I felt I couldn't afford to turn down the work I had lined up for At The Races and corporate box holders. I asked Richard if we could delay the operation. He said we could but only by a week. That told me all I needed to know. So did the look on Julie's face.

I have a long association with cancer. Dad died of it and Janie died of it but Bob Champion did not die of it. Right from the first time I told him what was going on, Bob was a great help. Nobody, however, is harder hit than the family. How do you tell your kids that their father is seriously ill? How do you explain to them what's happening? And if they ask you to promise them that you're going to be okay, what do you say? My solution came in two parts. I knew I had to be positive. Richard had made clear that we had caught it early. That could only be good news. I was basically a fit and healthy person, which would also be a big help. When I thought about the cancer I had lots of reasons to be optimistic. Even so, I tried my best not to think about it. Put it to the back of your mind, Tommo. The old way had always worked for me. Why shouldn't it work again?

There was one thing that did give me particular cause for concern. Richard had told me that after the operation I might have to wear a colostomy bag for the rest of my life. That frightened me. Richard even said that before I went under the knife I would be marked up for the bag, just in case it was needed. On the plus side, apparently there was only a three per cent chance of that happening. As a punter I know what odds that equates to, so the cards were stacked in my favour, but outsiders do sometimes oblige. I just hoped this one would not.

I'll never forget the day of the operation. The anaesthetist was a lovely South African guy, so we spoke about our shared interest in rugby and exchanged a few jokes. It took my mind off what was coming next – and what was coming next lasted much longer than anyone had expected. Richard told me after the operation that it took well over three hours before he could start tackling the cancer. When they opened me up he found a benign growth that was causing a massive blockage. 'How you've lived with that I do not know,' he told me, but evidently I had. Somehow I had survived the blockage. Now I had to survive the cancer.

I had come through what in total turned out to be a six-and-a-half-hour operation. In the few hours following surgery I wasn't completely sure it had been worth coming through it. I have never known pain like it and I hope that I'll never know pain like it again.

'How are you feeling?' Richard asked me when he did his rounds the following morning.

'Terrible,' I replied, but apparently that is to be expected. I couldn't move and I detested that. I hate not being in control and I had no control over what was happening to me at all. They gave me a device that has a button you can press to get painkillers into your body. I'm not ashamed to say that I pressed it a lot. I needed all the chemical help I could get.

In terms of medical care I was treated in a first-class manner, but I would be less than honest if I said that the nursing care was always what I had hoped and expected it would be. Everyone knows how stretched the NHS gets, so you make allowances, but there were times when I thought certain members of the caring profession did not seem to care. In the early days, at a time when I was hooked up to all manner of equipment, I asked a female nurse if I could possibly have a drink of water. She told me that the drinks trolley would be round in half an hour. 'Right,' I thought. 'That's helpful.' I had to stagger out of bed, walk across the ward and help myself to a glass of water. The thirst went but the sense of disappointment did not. After Julie had a word with one of the nursing team, the situation got a lot better.

On the positive side, I was in a ward full of nice people, some of whom knew who Tommo was, some of whom did not. Quite quickly, those who did not soon did. It felt as though they were on my side. All of us were pulling together, asking how each other felt, wishing each other well. For me, the big wish was that I would not be required to wear a bag. I wanted to remain in control of my number ones and twos but Richard made very clear what I needed to do to achieve that goal.

'I want you to pass wind within six days, otherwise you'll have to have a bag for the rest of your life,' he said.

I told him that would not be a problem. I've always been a really good farter so I couldn't see how producing a single trump over the course of six days was going to be difficult. But could I fart? Fart I could not. Not for ages. In fact, it was well into the sixth day, with the clock ticking down all too rapidly, that I finally managed one. It was only a little one, a tiny little trump, but I had done it. I had also opened the floodgates because almost as soon as fart number one had been successfully executed, fart number two followed quickly behind. This time it was a massive one, a real whopper, just like one of the farts that the Tommo of old had always been able to emit. All the guys in the ward cheered.

'I've farted guys!' I exclaimed, genuine delight in my voice. Then I rang Julie and said, 'Darling, I farted, I farted', and she was delighted as well. As moments of relief go, I've not had many bigger ones.

That was good but so much else of my time in hospital was bad, quite simply because I was in so much pain. I was barely able to eat anything and ended up losing two and a half stones. Just getting to the loo, which was only two yards away, was difficult. I had to be taught how to get out of bed and then practically taught how to walk again as well. It wasn't so much that I didn't know what to do. I did. I just didn't have the strength to do it. I was lucky as I got to work with a superb physiotherapist, who had a little box with three steps on it. It looked a bit like a mounting block that you use to get on a horse. Getting to the top of the box wouldn't get me on a horse but it would get me out of hospital. She told me that until I could climb all three steps I wouldn't be able to go home. The first time I tried I couldn't climb one step, let alone three. I was so desperate to go home that I returned to the gym in the middle of the night and tried as hard as I could to climb the mountain. I tried and tried and finally did it. The following morning, when the physiotherapist took me into the gym, I was able to get up the steps at the first time of asking. I was good to go.

But by then I knew I would have to return. Before the operation Richard told me that there was a chance I would need to undergo a course of chemotherapy afterwards. He said that for some patients it was deemed necessary, for others it was not. A few days after surgery he sat on the side of my bed and told me that the operation had been a total success but, to be completely on the safe side, he wanted me to have chemotherapy. He explained that he had got the bits that were there, but added there was no real knowing whether or not the problem might have spread. That was a blow. The thought of surgery had never been as frightening as the thought of chemotherapy. I had seen what torment the drugs had put Bob through. All the nightmares associated with that time came flooding back into my head. Richard was very up front with me and said that 30 per cent of patients choose to take the risk and not have chemotherapy. To me that never seemed like an attractive option. If chemotherapy was a sort of insurance policy, it was one I had to take. I wanted to be as sure as I could be that I was better, and if the chance of that coming true required chemotherapy then so be it.

Between surgery and chemotherapy there was a break. It took about a month before I was properly recovered from the operation and Richard wanted to give my body another additional month of recovery before treatment began. I approached it with trepidation. The doctors always tell you they can never be sure how a body will react to chemotherapy. Some people handle it better than others but you can never be certain beforehand which group you'll fall into. I had been assured that I wouldn't lose my hair, which was good to know, but I feared I would be little more than a zombie for the six months that I was due to be in and out of Addenbrooke's.

But then I had some good news. I was commentating one day when I was approached by David Higgins, a friend and owner with Paul Webber who works for a top insurance company in the city. He knocked on the door of the commentary box, we started chatting and he asked if I knew he had been treated for cancer the previous year. I didn't know that, but I was heartened to see he looked so well and also that he told me he had worked through chemotherapy. He suggested that for someone like me, working through it might be a real help. I couldn't have agreed more. I had been forced to take off much of the month that followed the operation, and although all my regular employers were absolutely outstanding through the illness, I wanted to work not just for them but for me. To me, working is like breathing. Without it, I find it hard to function. I told myself that chemotherapy was not only going to help me, it was also not going to stop me from earning a crust. And it didn't. But my goodness, to work was very hard work indeed.

With chemotherapy the routine is, in theory, the same every time. In my case, I would go into hospital on the morning of the appointment and have a blood sample taken. You wait a while for the doctor to make sure that your blood seems fine. If it is, the drugs are ordered. You then go away for a while because nobody wants to be in hospital if they don't have to be, before returning in the afternoon for treatment.

If any of you ever find yourself in this position – and some of you are bound to – please do not be alarmed. There is nothing scary, depressing or even clinical about a chemotherapy ward. At Addenbrooke's there were two largish rooms full of beds and comfortable chairs. You choose where you want to go, you get attached to a drip and fluids are flushed through your system prior to the drugs being administered in the same way. It really isn't hard. The worst part, in theory, could be boredom, as you can be sat there for two to three hours twiddling your thumbs. You need to be sure that you have something to do. And I did. I worked. When I was having the treatment I would go through my diary, fixing up dates, making appointments, doing my level best to make sure there were no blanks to be seen. When the drugs are all in your body you go home and get told to take anti-sickness medication if needed. For me it was never needed.

It takes a while for the effects of chemotherapy to kick in. After the first course I didn't really feel that bad at all. I was lulled into a false sense of security. Following the second set of drugs I received a reality check. Soon enough, I felt terrible and I looked terrible as well. People who saw me received a bit of a shock. I looked gaunt. I looked ill. I looked old. I was constantly tired and most nights would be in bed by eight o'clock in the evening. I felt as though I had either gone 15 rounds with a world heavy-weight champion or drunk far too much red wine. After a while my hands started to feel strange. A sensation something akin to pins and needles filled my veins. The ends of my fingers felt per-manently frozen. My feet followed suit. I had two icy blocks at the ends of my legs and regularly went to bed wearing two pairs of socks. I looked and felt like death warmed up. But I never stopped working.

Sometimes it was very difficult. Bob was great and often drove me wherever I had to be, but on other occasions I drove myself to make sure I kept my mind alert. Thankfully German motoring technology was a big help. I have no idea how it does this, but my Mercedes can sense if I'm getting drowsy. If it thinks I'm putting myself or others at risk it instructs me to pull over and have a coffee. I ended up having an awful lot of coffee when going up and down Britain's motorways. Throughout the process I was determined not to be beaten and if someone offered me a job I was equally determined to take it. I remember one chemotherapy day in particular. I went to Addenbrooke's in the morning for the blood tests. In between getting that done and being given the drugs in the afternoon I opened a betting shop in Huntingdon. That's me. Why waste two hours if you don't need to?

I did, however, have some natural assistance in the form of Middle Eastern sunshine. In between chemotherapy sessions I was supposed to fly out to Dubai to do one of my presenting shifts at Jebel Ali. I was told not to go by the doctors. It was also explained to me that it would be impossible to get any insurance cover for all the time I was out there. Luckily, I was sure that Jebel Ali's owner Sheikh Ahmed would have flown me home on his private jet if there had been a problem. I wanted to go not only because there was a job waiting there for me, but also because I was convinced the sunshine would do me good, which it did. Orange juice is so expensive at home but when you're staying in a hotel it's all included so I was filling myself up with vitamin C every morning. If there was health food, a health drink or a piece of fruit to be seen I had it. I shovelled down as much as I could and then returned home feeling in considerably better shape. That feeling did not last long.

I had chemotherapy on Christmas Eve, which went fine, but the next session in mid-January did not go so well. I can't explain why, but I felt apprehensive heading to the hospital. I just wasn't feeling right, but I put the thoughts to the back of my mind. By the time I got into the ward I was on more of an even kilter but I could tell there was a problem after only about two minutes of the drugs going in. Both my hands started to get hotter and hotter until it reached the point that they were burning. Then my feet started going the same way. They were on fire. My feet were on fire and my hands were on fire. I was on fire. Then I was dizzy. I felt sick, both nauseous sick and ill sick. The lovely male South African nurse came over to me and asked if I was all right. I told him that I wasn't. By now I was becoming breathless as well.

The nurse brought me a plastic bowl to be sick in but by now sickness was just one of many things consuming my body. Sweat had started dripping off me. I felt close to collapse. I heard another nurse shouting that I needed to be moved from the chair. I was taken to a bed instead. Someone said to remove the drugs. I heard someone else say, 'he's rejecting it', but I don't remember hearing much more. In my increasingly confused head there was sound but there were no words. An oxygen mask was placed over my face. There must have been six nurses and two doctors stood around the bed. It was like I was a central character in an episode of *Casualty*, which would have been somehow appropriate as its longest-serving cast member, the one who plays Charlie Fairhead, is called Derek Thompson. If there was any point in the whole cancer episode when I felt I might die, this was it. It was terrible.

When I came round I saw Bob at the end of the bed. 'What a lot of trouble you've been causing,' he said. You can always rely on Champ to lighten the mood. Thank goodness he did.

The staff at Addenbrooke's had been wonderful. My body had rejected the drugs, which can happen sometimes, and the way I had reacted was apparently perfectly normal. I was told I would feel much better the following day, but it was more like four or five days before I was really like the Tommo who had gone into hospital feeling anxious that January morning. What really disappointed me was the night after my incident I had a long-standing dinner engagement with Michael Howard, the former Home Secretary and leader of the Conservative Party, and his wife Sandra in the House of Lords. Michael is the chairman of Britain's biggest racecourse group, the Arena Racing Company, and I like him a lot. He had also invited the legendary former trainer Michael Dickinson and his wife Joan, plus the top jumps owner Andy Stewart and his wife Judy. Julie had been looking forward to it as well but there was no way I could go, so I had to ring Michael and apologise. I'm sure it was a wonderful night but the way I was feeling I would have been terrible company.

After the drugs rejection I was placed on pills instead. They left me absolutely whacked out but I carried on and somehow continued to work. I once spoke about it to the man who would be crowned champion jockey, Richard Hughes. He asked me how I was doing, and I explained that when I was working I was okay but then as soon as I got home I was exhausted.

'Adrenaline,' he said. 'It's the best drug in the world.'

And do you know what? Hughesie was right.

I no longer have cancer. I got the all-clear in the spring of 2013 and now just have to hope the cancer doesn't return.

At no point did I receive any counselling because at no point did I think any was needed. I wanted to survive and I did survive. That's good enough for me. I know some people will think I was mad to work throughout the treatment process, but it was my way of coping. My most important job always has been, and always will be, to provide for my family. One of the thoughts in my mind

224

when I began to tackle cancer was that I wanted, at the very least, to have got both India and Hugo through school. You have to have goals. That is one of my mine and I intend to see it through.

At no point did I get angry. I couldn't see what good anger would do me. Nor did Julie and I ever discuss the possibility of me dying. In fact I don't think I discussed it with anybody. Now that I've come through the other side, my brother Howard keeps telling me to make sure that after all we've been through I don't get run over by a bus. Good attitude that. If you don't laugh, you cry.

And I genuinely think you have to be positive. Where at all possible, look on the bright side. Part of me now thinks that it was a good thing I had cancer. Thanks to the screening process you enjoy after having had it once, there's a great chance that if it ever comes back it will be detected almost immediately. That has to be a good thing.

I think you almost have to embrace cancer and say to yourself: 'Okay, I've got this thing. What can I make it do for me?'

I'll tell you what it can do. It can bring out the best in you and make you a better person. It makes you realise how much you love those who mean the most to you. It can conjure up from within you a fighting spirit that you might have not known you had. And it makes you see how much better life is than the alternative.

It can also make you see people in a different light. I remember the *Racing Post* journalist David Ashforth once wrote a profile on me that I thought was needlessly cruel, but David continues to go through cancer himself and he wrote me a lovely letter that made me think of him as a friend, not an enemy.

Not everyone will survive cancer, but you shouldn't treat it as a death sentence because it doesn't have to be one. I still get tired more than I used to, and I do get irritable and snappy because of that, but it's a price well worth paying in the circumstances. Sometimes I do feel as though I'm mentally flagging, but physically I generally feel great, no doubt in part because I now eat much more healthily.

The former world snooker champion, Peter Ebdon, is a good mate and someone who has gained a serious interest in cancer treatment since the death of his father, Michael, from the disease in May 2011. Peter has done considerable research into diet, nutrition and cancer, and has come to the conclusion that a vegan, whole foods, plant based, high carbohydrate, low protein, low fat, no salt diet is best for both the prevention and treatment of cancer, and indeed any other degenerative condition. Peter strongly recommends not eating processed foods, including anything from a packet, tin or jar. He is also adamant that it is absolutely imperative that our food intake should consist of as much organic produce as possible and that it should also include fresh, organic fruit and vegetable juices, made with a juicer and blender. Peter, a genuinely decent guy, wrote to me and offered all the advice you've just read. I haven't yet managed to adopt it all completely, but I do now largely follow his recommendations. But for having cancer I would still have been stuffing cholesterol-laden pies and chips down my face. Now I'm all about salads, fruits and vegetables. I very seldom eat red meat, which so many people in the know are convinced is a cause of bowel cancer, and instead go for fish and chicken. The barbecue has gone as well, thrown away because it is no longer needed. At long last I'm treating my body like a temple. Cancer might even have helped me to live longer!

So many other people wrote to me offering advice, some good, some not so good, some of which I took, some of which I did not. Having tried various different products, and listened to considerable different pieces of advice, I would certainly recommend turmeric capsules. A vital ingredient in turmeric is curcumin, which scientists think is useful in fending off cancer. Also worth trying are selenium capsules, which contain a powerful antioxidant, and a product called Super Green Energy Drink, which gives you your five a day in one hit and is beloved of rugby players.

One particular rugby player, my son Jim, was wonderful through my illness, as was his brother Alex. They were great but then all my family were great. Julie is a wonderful woman, the most caring and compassionate lady I've ever met. She doesn't mind telling me when I've gone wrong, which I do now and again, but she is my most ardent supporter and could not have been more magnificent throughout the illness. India and Hugo helped their old dad get through it, and mum and Howard were as dependable and loving as ever. So, too, was my smashing brother-in-law David Summerfield and his partner Zoe. They have no connections to horseracing but David has a link to horsepower as for the last 20 years he has had a repair garage in the Arundel stables for so long occupied by John Dunlop. I am blessed with family but also with friends and Champ in particular could not have done more for me.

Nor was he alone in offering unflinching backing. When I was going through a rough patch I received a get-well card from the leading jumps owner Ged Mason and his racing partner Sir Alex Ferguson. Both Ged and Sir Alex have been tremendous supporters and their kindness helped a great deal. I felt the same when I got a touching text message from the astonishingly brave jump jockey Christian Williams, who I think at the time could barely use either of his arms after a series of operations. My very good mate Mike Morris and his wife Michelle, an ex-nurse, have been the most tremendous allies and were always there for me They also part-owned that excellent sprinter Deacon Blues and in various ways have been as good to racing as they have to me. I also received lots of encouragement from Carlo, the restaurant maitre d' at all the best racecourses. Carlo, who is so good that like Madonna and Adele he only needs the one name, is now fighting cancer himself but he has the right spirit to beat it. I've no doubt that Carlo is also getting the sort of backing that helped me so much when I was ill and when I was better. After I got the all-clear I received more than a thousand congratulatory messages on Twitter. They reduced me to tears but for all the right reasons. People I've never met were genuinely pleased for me. People were there for me at the beginning of cancer, at its middle and at its end.

Inevitably it helps to speak with people who are going through the same thing as you. Sadly, there were all too many people in that position. One of them was the multiple champion jumps owner David Johnson. David was an inspirational figure. He once told me about a time when he was trying to raise money for a project. He went to a bank for a loan. The bank turned him down so David bought the bank instead! David was that sort of person. He turned negatives into positives. He had a can-do attitude and he refused to let cancer ruin his life, even if cancer eventually took that life. He was exceptionally kind and supportive to me and I wanted in this book to record my gratitude to him on paper. David left us in July this year but all those who loved him and counted him as a friend have been left with so many happy memories.

Like David, Sir Henry Cecil refused to let cancer dictate how he would live his life. I remember one morning on the gallops, a few weeks after the operation and before my treatment had started.

Henry made a point of coming over and talking to me. He was going through the same thing himself, only much worse, but by the time he saw me I had lost an awful lot of weight and so clearly did not look well.

'How's it going?' he asked me, his voice barely strong enough to be heard. I told him and then for ten minutes we had a lovely heart-to-heart conversation, squatting down on Warren Hill because the grass was too wet for us to sit on. He told me what to expect, how it would hurt, how it would affect me and how I should approach it. 'We need to remain positive, you have to remain positive,' he said. I went back to the house and told Julie that I had just had one of the most amazing ten minutes of my life. That was all down to Henry.

Later in the year, after Frankel won the Juddmonte International at York, Andrew Franklin told me in my ear that we had to get an interview with Henry.

'Boss, he can barely talk,' I said. I felt a bit awkward asking, but I went across to Henry and spoke to him in the same hushed tones he had been reduced to himself.

'If I speak to you like this, would you mind talking to me on Channel 4?' I asked.

'Yes,' he said. 'If we can talk like this, let's do it.' He then gave me one of the best interviews of my career. Many people have also told me that although Henry could not say a lot, they had never seen him give a better interview. It was one of my proudest moments. I don't think I have often felt a bond with an inter-viewee as much as I did that day. I asked Henry how Frankel's win had made him feel. In three simple words he summed it up beautifully: 'Twenty years better.'

Very sadly, in June 2013 he passed away. He was an incredible man. He could at times be frustrating but he was also one of the most loveable and likeable men you could ever meet. He is greatly missed, but since his death the name Cecil has continued to win races – including at Royal Ascot – thanks to his wife Jane, who helped him so valiantly throughout his illness and deserves endless credit.

And in some ways that's central to the key message I want to put out. Large chunks of my life have been about stuff and nonsense because that's what large chunks of everyone's lives are about. The tough times are what matter most and it's when you are confronted with dying that you think most about living. Cancer is not pleasant, and I'm not going to pretend otherwise, but I'm sure that many of us who have had it would say that it's actually the loved ones of the person who has cancer who really suffer most. When you're going through chemotherapy, radiotherapy or whatever treatment you've been prescribed, you just have to get on with it. Unless you want to wave the white flag and surrender, you don't really have much choice. You just have to take the drugs, deal with the exhaustion and wait for a brighter tomorrow. In most cases it's not really a case of you bravely fighting to live, more that you're attempting to stave off the alternative. Those who are caring for you, loving you and worrying about you deserve the most credit as they are the ones who get you to the other end. I know that was the case with me.

And if you're lucky you will pull through. If you're reading this and you have cancer yourself, you have my very best wishes. The statistics show the odds are in your favour. You can do it. With all my heart I hope that you do.

NINETEEN

WHAT I DO

I am almost certainly the only man in history ever to complete the treble of commentating on synchronised swimming at an Olympic Games, calling a Grand National and being Gotcha'd by Noel Edmonds. I'm not even sure anybody else ever has ever done two of the three. Why it hasn't got me in the *Guinness Book of Records* I've no idea.

I love to work and I live to work. One of the reasons I love it so much is that I have such a variety of jobs. One of the reasons I have such a variety of jobs is that I work so much. You name it, I've probably done it, and I probably still do. Being a jack of all trades might have cost me the number-one job with Channel 4 when Brough Scott retired, but it's something that has also kept me busy and in demand throughout my working life.

In an earlier chapter I said that my favourite Channel 4 race meeting was always the one that was coming next. I'm a bit the same with work in general. I always look forward to whatever is next in my diary. There is, however, something that affects me in a different way to anything else I do, and yet in some ways is the thing I have been doing for longest. Commentating terrifies me.

I was only a teenager when I first took the microphone from my father at our local point-to-point and I was only 23 when I described Red Rum cutting into Crisp's lead in the 1973 Grand National. Forty years later, you can still hear me describing the start, middle and end of races up and down the country. It's something I'm keen to carry on doing for as long as I possibly can – and I was extremely upset when it looked as though the job might be snatched from my grasp in 2011. Even so, nothing scares me like calling the horses.

There was a long spell when I did not do it. When I worked for BBC Radio in the early years of my broadcasting career I commentated on plenty of races. I was part of the team for eight consecutive Grand Nationals and whenever Peter Bromley was on holiday or ill I took his place. When I joined ITV things changed. ITV had more than enough commentators of its own with Graham Goode, Raleigh Gilbert and John Penney already on the books. All three moved across to Channel 4, for whom I was needed more than anything as a presenter and reporter. Commentating was something I had to put to one side. An offer that came from out of the blue in 1986 made me reconsider the situation.

George Irvine, a great mate for many years, invited me to lunch and told me he was involved in the creation of a new company, Satellite Information Services, that was going to broadcast racing pictures into betting shops for the first time. Previously only commentaries were heard but SIS was set to change all that. Essentially it was going to provide a TV channel for betting shops and George, who had worked his way up through the bookmaking industry having once been a betting shop manager, wanted me on exclusive terms to be the channel's face. It was a flattering offer, and I can't say I wasn't tempted, but I rejected the overture for the same reason I turned down the offer to relocate to Dubai and become Sheikh Mohammed's main media man. I wanted to stay with Channel 4. Not many people say no to Sheikh Mohammed and SIS. I am the man that did.

But even though I politely passed up the chance to work exclusively for SIS, I did prick my ears at another idea that George put forward. In those days there was a division between the commentaries that were played out in betting shops and the commentaries heard on racecourses. George asked me if I would like to be one of the SIS shop commentators. I jumped at the chance and soon enough became a regular voice in betting offices up and down the land. When the two jobs were later combined, I became the soundtrack to scores of race meetings every year, my voice being heard on the track, in the shops and, when the dedicated racing channels began broadcasting, on them as well. As both Raleigh and John retired, I also started to do some commentary work for Channel 4, standing in when GG or Simon Holt were not available. On top of all that, I was the man behind the mike at Nad Al Sheba, bringing the Tommo tones to the first Dubai World Cup, not to mention Dubai Millennium's iconic victory in the same race.

Commentating has given me some great days but nothing I do is harder work and nothing brings with it such a large burden of pressure. Presenting is easy. Give me a microphone and I can fill as much air time as a director needs. Sometimes the words come out the wrong way but they always come out. There isn't really a right or a wrong. With commentating there is. The fear of getting it wrong is always there and even with years of experience behind me it's there all the time. In fact, as you get more experienced you inevitably also get older, and I've found that getting older means you need to do more homework, preparation and research in order to get it right.

There are commentators like Ian Bartlett who can have a quick peek at a racecard and then call a 25-runner race flawlessly. I'm not like that. If I'm commentating I get up even earlier than usual. I do my own card for every race, using felt-tip pens to colour in the silks of every horse in the race. If it's a Flat meeting I make sure I put the colours together in draw order. As I'm drawing I'm also learning, trying to get the names of all the horses inextricably linked in my brain with the silks their jockeys will be wearing. Julie hates the time it takes me and she hates me commentating. I do my preparation at home but I might as well not be there. I have to ignore everything and everyone while I do it, including her, India and Hugo. For the same reason, Julie loathes going racing with me when I'm commentating. If I'm presenting or doing Tommo TV it's fine. I am completely in my comfort zone. Not so when I'm commentating. They say fear concentrates the mind. I would absolutely agree.

Inevitably it sometimes goes wrong. It once did for me in a major way when I called the wrong winner at Lingfield. For a commentator, it's the equivalent of a jockey riding a finish a circuit too soon or easing up just before the line and throwing away a race. I had done my homework but I had made what turned out to be the fatal mistake of not putting together my colours chart in draw order. That cost me dear. It's very rare indeed that people will say anything after you've given a good call, but get one wrong and the vultures come out. Even if they didn't you would beat yourself into an emotional pulp. I know I did. Heading home that night I wanted to drive the car into a lamppost. I honestly felt as though I wanted to kill myself. It was that bad. Yet I have carried on doing it and don't want to stop.

I do have my own way of doing things. For a start I don't use binoculars. I always have binoculars with me but only as a back-up in case something goes wrong with the monitor. The vast majority of people watching any race I commentate on will be viewing it on television. Even most people on the racecourse will be relying on the big screen. On the basis that such people are the biggest part of the audience, I work around them. That doesn't mean I forget about the people in the stands. My modus operandi, as with everything I do, is to make it entertaining. Obviously the call needs to be accurate, and I'm one of those commentators who goes out of his way to point out the colours a jockey is wearing while I'm describing a race. However, you can't just call a race in a regimented way. I am nothing if not enthusiastic and I try to bring that to the commentary box. Catchphrases, I've found, are a big help.

Some come and go, others have stood the test of time. I used to say, 'who's gonna get there?', quite a lot, but I tend not to use that so much these days. Whenever I call the former champion jockey Paul Hanagan I like to refer to him as 'Hanagan the managan', and I do love a close finish as I'm very fond of exclaiming: 'That's a photo!' I like to give the word 'photo' a real bit of oomph and people seem to like that. If it really does look too close to call, I follow it up with: 'We'll leave that one to the judge' or 'that's one for the judge'. I must have left that one to the judge thousands of times over the years.

Sometimes the catchphrases become part of my everyday life. I remember I brought my sons Alex and James to Leicester one day while they were still young boys. They had stayed in the racecourse press box – probably eating all the sandwiches – while I called what turned out to be a head-bobbing finish. When I got down to the box one of the boys asked me which horse had won.

'Son,' I said. 'We'll have to leave that one to the judge.'

The press guys seemed to find that funny.

Another of my most-used lines has concerned Frankie Dettori. When I can see him making a move on a horse I have often said, with no little Tommo excitement: 'Here comes Frankie!' That always goes down well, especially on Friday nights at Newmarket. For reasons I could never understand, RaceTech, the company that now oversees the employment of commentators, asked me why I mention Frankie so much. I explained it's because he is the most famous and easily recognisable jockey in the world. That didn't seem to wash with them and they asked me to reduce the Frankie references, which I thought was strange. It was not, however, the strangest thing RaceTech has said to me.

It was widely reported that late in 2011 RaceTech informed four commentators – Jim McGrath, Darren Owen, Iain Mackenzie and myself – that they were being placed on a six-month review by the Commentators User Group, a body comprising representatives of RaceTech, the Racecourse Association, Racing UK, TurfTV, At The Races and SIS. RaceTech was furious that it had been reported by anyone. They thought nobody would say anything, so after Jim, or the Croc as everyone knows him, talked about it to the *Racing Post*, RaceTech wrote to us all saying that if anyone made a public comment during the review process that person's contract would be terminated. That seemed pretty scandalous to me, but just as bad was the fact that when I rang the RaceTech boss Brad Higgins and asked what it was that members of the CUG wanted me to do differently, he said he could not tell me. He also couldn't tell me which members of the group were unhappy with my performance. How can you tell four experienced professionals that they need to improve but not also say in what way?

I know Jim was livid and rightly so. This was the man the BBC employed to commentate on the finish of the Grand National to an audience of ten million people in Britain alone, and yet some in the CUG were apparently dubious about whether he was fit to commentate on a seller at Southwell. Darren was another member of the BBC's Aintree team, Iain had years of experience behind him and I was Tommo. None of us could get our heads around it, but for six months we were placed under extreme pressure. Julie was especially furious and contemplated taking legal advice. Fortunately in the end I was retained. Darren still commentates as well, but Iain did not return in 2013 and Jim announced his retirement from calling in Britain just before the latest Royal Ascot. His voice will be much missed.

Even without the stress the review process caused, I reckon commentating has taken ten years off my life. Julie reckons it's taken ten years off hers as well! It's a nerve-racking thing to do but I get an enormous buzz from it. I was given plenty of dates for this year and was even asked by Newmarket to become the permanent voice of the July course, which I unfortunately wasn't able to do. I simply had too many other commitments, which in some ways was a shame – by now you must know how much I hate to turn down a job!

Not everyone reckons I'm the greatest judge in the world but for years there were plenty of people prepared to pay by the minute to hear my selections every day of the week.

Thanks to some nice people at BT, then still British Telecom, I was asked if I would like to start up a telephone tipping line of my own. I agreed and I was glad that I did. Through the 1980s the Tommo Hotlines proved extremely lucrative. They practically paid to put Alex and James through school. Some people, especially John McCririck, hated the very idea of a tipping line but nobody forced anybody to ring them and anybody who did had it made very clear to them what a call was going to cost per minute. It wasn't even as though I was raking in the majority of what the lines were earning. The line provider always got the lion's share and I only really received a small percentage of what was left after everyone else had gobbled up their slice of the pie. That said, during the heyday of the lines, my slice was enough to prevent me from getting hungry.

Over time the popularity of telephone tipping lines waned, not surprisingly so given how much they cost to ring. I complained about the cost angle but there was nothing I could do. These days I work with the former champion jump jockey Richard Dunwoody on a line but what that brings in is very little compared to everything else that I do. Even so, I still think I was pretty useful at finding winners, even if there was one very unfortunate occasion when a newspaper pitted me in a tipping challenge against a West Highland terrier called Steptoe. You've guessed right. The dog won. He clearly had a gift for it.

Yet while the tipping lines no longer form a big part of my working life, betting shops very much do and I try to open at least one a week. I travel up and down the country bringing my own brand of Tommo magic and a copious number of free bets to shops in every corner of the country. I love it because I love people and I certainly love betting shops, their punters and their staff. If there is a shop that is being opened or re-opened and I'm not the one doing the opening or re-opening, I feel as though I've failed. It's a little niche I created for myself many years ago and I'd like to think it works as well for the bookmakers as it does for me. Many of the shops I open are for William Hill, so to Natalie and John in the bookmaker's public relations department, thanks very much indeed!

Something that also works well for bookmakers – and one bookmaker in particular – is Tommo TV. It obviously also works for the racecourses who employ me or I wouldn't get the bookings. The idea came a few years ago, once again following a meeting with George Irvine. My shifts for Channel 4 were drying up and I was missing proper racecourse work. George, who knows broadcasting and bookmaking like the back of his hand, suggested that I front what would effectively be my own TV channel during a day at the races. He said: 'You do the presenting, I'll provide the cameras and we'll call it Tommo TV.' And we did!

These days Tommo TV might be at a racecourse near you up to twice a week. Imagine that! Most of the Arena Racing Company tracks use me, for which I'm very grateful to the boss Tony Kelly, who has a huge job but does it brilliantly. Thanks to the ARC association I'm often at places like Doncaster, Lingfield, Fontwell and Uttoxeter, whose executive director David MacDonald is just about the most progressive racecourse manager in the country and always seems to manage to get the track full of happy customers.

Another of my regular ARC tracks is Wolverhampton, at which Dave Roberts is a tremendous managing director, while I'm never less than happy to visit Sedgefield, where the general manager Jill Williamson does sterling work. I'm very much a regular at Musselburgh, whose outstanding chief executive Bill Farnsworth has been one of my biggest supporters, and I also spend a lot of time at Hamilton, which is run by the excellent Hazel Peplinski. You'll see Tommo TV at Aintree and Haydock, down the road from me at Newmarket, a bit further down the road at Huntingdon, and also once a year at York, where the two main men William Derby and James Brennan are excellent. If you're at one of those racecourses on one of my days, you'll hear my voice throughout the afternoon or evening. I try to keep people interested, I make the experience entertaining and also, I'd like to think, informative. On top of that, if a racecourse has a few tables still to sell in a restaurant, I'll take my cameraman up to the restaurant and do my best to get those missing bums on the empty seats.

I know this is something I say a lot, but I love it. I really do. The Tote has always been a big backer of Tommo TV and they saw its merit when they realised how much betting turnover was increasing at the meetings I was doing. I'm pleased to say that the Tote's racecourse commercial manager Ben Turnbull is still an enthusiastic fan of Tommo TV and helps to keep it on air. I'm delighted he does because there was one day at Musselburgh when betting turnover increased year on year by 44 per cent with the incredible rise attributed to Tommo TV. The racecourse bookies love it for the same reason. I even try to give a new interest to those people whose bets have lost. One of the best things I've brought to the world is Tommo's Lucky Bucket. It dawned on me that why should the loss of a horse be the end of your betting experience with that horse. Wouldn't it be great if we could make a losing bet a winning bet? I thought that was a stroke of genius. What I do, in my usual understated way, is get on the microphone and tell punters to stick their losing betting tickets in my lucky bucket and then we draw out a few in the winner's enclosure. The people whose tickets get drawn out win free bets. Magic!

There are times when a Tommo TV broadcast includes a very special added extra – a best-dressed lady competition. I love them and have done a lot of them. Every one I go to is the best in the country, or at least it is for that day. The following day, whichever one I'm at becomes the best in the country. By saying that, it makes the ladies feel special, and if Tommo can make the ladies feel special he is a happy man.

I should probably have given over this section of the book to Julie, because I'm very proud to say that my wife is not just incredibly brainy but also incredibly beautiful. When I attached myself to Julie I hooked up with a stunner. For three years in a row she was the winner of the prestigious best-dressed lady competition at Doncaster's St Leger meeting. She was the Arkle or Red Rum of the discipline, although in some ways her achievements were even greater because being named the best-dressed lady at Doncaster is even harder than winning the Gold Cup or Grand National.

I should stress that I am generally only the host, not a judge. I am to racecourse best-dressed lady competitions what my old mate Judith Chalmers was to Miss World. However, because I am on duty at so many of the competitions I can give the girls a bit of advice. Tommo's mantra would be to make sure you get your colour co-ordination right. Also be as stylish as you can possibly afford without wearing something you think another girl might have on as well. Accessorise yourself elegantly with lovely shoes and a nice handbag and don't be afraid of second hand shops. I know I never have been. So many of the ladies who win these competitions have done so wearing what were once other people's clothes.

I'm glad to say that it shouldn't really matter what you look like. It obviously helps if you're beautiful, and it certainly did Julie no harm when she was mopping up at Donny, but looks aren't everything. Come along wearing a nice frock and you never know what might happen. Having said that, I have suggested to some racecourses that there should sometimes be two competitions, one for the best-dressed lady and one for the most revealingly dressed lady. There are definitely men out there who prefer the trashy, tarty, tacky look, and plenty of us would pay good money to attend a competition in which the girls were dressed in miniskirts. Julie thinks it's a terrible idea but Julie wouldn't be the target audience.

Some of my most enjoyable and unusual racecourse moments have been spent watching ladies performing before judges. We get all sorts of different people, which is part of the attraction. At Brighton we once had a couple of cross-dressers, which was nice, and at Huntingdon the other day we had a bank manager. I thought that was incredible and it just shows how far the world has come. I always ask the girls, what's your name and where do you come from, in the way Cilla did on *Blind Date*, and on this day a particularly vivacious individual said: 'Hi Tommo, I'm

Mandy, I'm from Ely and I'm a bank manager.' I couldn't believe it. She looked like someone you would meet down the local disco but she actually did the same job as Captain Mainwaring in *Dad's Army*. I asked her for a loan.

There was also a decidedly unfortunate event at Fontwell. The judge had failed to turn up and I thought that instead of judging it myself I should get one of the racegoers to do it. I reckoned that could be comedy gold. A few hands went up, as you'd expect, and I went for a pretty nondescript-looking guy, as I thought he looked like the sort of person who would appreciate something good happening to him for a change. We stood together and moved along the line of ten ladies, asking them the usual questions, until it got to the point when a decision had to be made.

'Come on then, who's it going to be?' I asked, reminding him that the chosen one would win £1,000. That got an 'ooohh' from the audience.

Unbelievably, he picked the dowdiest-looking woman you will ever see. I don't even know how she got into the final ten. If you had been a bookmaker you would have chalked up 100-1 against her winning. I couldn't get my head around it. Afterwards I asked him why he had picked her. He said she was his wife. I never did it that way again.

That incident was a bit embarrassing. So, too, was the time I tried to boost audience interaction. I said we would judge the competition on applause. The first girl got a massive cheer and so did the second, but when we got to the third entrant, a slightly plain-looking lady, there was nothing. Not a thing. 'Never mind,' I said, 'I think you're lovely,' doing my best to make her feel better. I think it worked but I didn't do it like that again. You live and you learn.

As you might have gathered by now, I do try to keep myself busy. As an example of how busy, here was what I had in my diary for June 2013:

June 1:   Musselburgh, hosting Tommo TV
June 2:   Fakenham, commentating
June 3:   Salford, Betfred TV
June 4:   Yarmouth, commentating
June 5:   Toulouse, 4am start, drive to Heathrow then to France for Arab Racing Conference
June 6:   Toulouse, hosting conference
June 7:   Toulouse, racecourse presenting and commentary
June 8:   Edinburgh, business meeting
June 9:   Betting shop openings (two)
June 10:   Milton Keynes, presenting for At The Races, then after-dinner speech in London
June 11:   Betting shop opening (one)
June 12:   Yarmouth, commentating, then London for Playboy Club Royal Ascot preview
June 13:   Salford, Betfred TV
June 14:   Musselburgh, hosting Tommo TV
June 15:   Musselburgh, hosting Tommo TV
June 16:   London, after-dinner speaking
June 17:   Salford, Betfred TV
June 18:   Royal Ascot, At The Races, corporate box speeches
June 19:   Royal Ascot, corporate box speeches

June 20:	Royal Ascot, corporate box speeches
June 21:	Royal Ascot, corporate box speeches
June 22:	Haydock, corporate box speeches
June 23:	Amsterdam, MC at Arab Racing gala dinner
June 24:	Amsterdam, racecourse presenting and commentary
June 25:	Amsterdam, hosting press conference
June 26:	Salford, Betfred TV
June 27:	Hamilton, Tommo TV
June 28:	Yarmouth, commentary
June 29:	Lingfield, Tommo TV
June 30:	Uttoxeter, Tommo TV

You'll see from the diary extract that even without Channel 4 I don't have much time to get bored, especially as Fred Done, the Betfred boss, and his PR executive Mark Pearson are now good enough to use me in Salford around once a week for the service that gets played into his company's betting shops. Dedicated betting shop channels like that show how much the industry is changing and I always have to be ready to react to that. It means that I haven't recently been able to do something I always used to enjoy, giving speeches on cruise ships, but there just aren't enough days in the week and the problem with a cruise ship is that it tends to stay on water for days on end. Mind you, if they ever start opening betting shops on ships I'll be ready and waiting!

I'm not exactly ready and waiting for a call from Channel 4, but as I've said before, my love for *Channel 4 Racing* is such that I would go back if and when they feel a relaunch would benefit from my services. It's not even as if I've been completely absent from the new-look *Channel 4 Racing* as commentating brought me back to the afternoon programme in May 2013. As a cost-cutting measure, Channel 4 does not pay for a commentator at its second-site meeting and has to take the call of whoever is providing the racecourse commentary. At Newmarket on this particular Saturday that was me. I bet that went down well with the Channel 4 bosses!

But although I might not have the best relationships with those who run *Channel 4 Racing*, I would still be good mates with most of those who work on the programme. In fact, I would like to think I have good relationships with most of the people I work with, regardless of who I'm working for at the time. I try not to fall out with people, so it saddened me that Big Mac so took against me. Even so, I can still see the good in him, as I can in most people, although it's no secret that my At The Races colleague Matt Chapman and I are not massive fans of each other. What's important, though, is that you can work with someone professionally, even when you don't get on with them personally. I have done that with Mac, Matt and also Ted Walsh, who I worked with for Channel 4 at so many Cheltenham Festivals. My relationship with Ted soured after he was very rude to me as a result of a question I asked his son, Ruby, following the 2008 Gold Cup, in which he picked Kauto Star over stablemate Denman and then watched from Kauto's back as Denman won under Sam Thomas. After the race, I asked Ruby live on air whether he had regretted choosing Kauto. I thought it was a perfectly fair question but Ruby responded by saying it was the most stupid question he had ever been asked. Personally, I thought that was extremely rude and discourteous of him, but it made for good television. Sometimes the job of the interviewer is to elicit a strong response from the interviewee and that's what my question did. It brought to the surface his frustration and disappointment at having been on 'the wrong one', but Ted didn't see it that way and had a real go at me once the programme was over. I was deeply disappointed in Ted. He is a trainer but he is also a broadcaster and he should have been able to see things from both sides of the fence. My respect for him is much less now than it used to be, and it reduced even more when Ted, in his role as an RTE pundit, mercilessly tore into Sam Waley-Cohen after he won the 2012 King George VI Chase on Long Run. Given that Sam had won the race I thought Ted's comments were needlessly harsh, especially as Ted wasn't saying what he said to Sam face to face. At least when I asked Ruby the Kauto question I had the courage to do it while stood right next to him.

I got to ask Ruby many more questions face to face at the latest Cheltenham Festival when I returned to my roots and worked there as part of the BBC Radio 5 live team. It was like coming home. When I was told late in 2012 that I would not be needed by Channel 4 one of the saddest aspects for me was the realisation that I probably would have no broadcasting work at the biggest meeting of the year. To have been there and felt like a spare part would have been awful. It was a real blow but then the phone rang and the offer came in to return to the BBC. Apparently the head of sport had asked his team who they wanted to replace Clare Balding, who had moved to Channel 4, and they all said Tommo. This moved me to tears. Nobody from the BBC had asked me back for more than 30 years. I was wanted again.

I flew into Cheltenham on the morning of the festival because I'd been working in Houston for Sheikh Mansour over the previous few days. From the airport it was straight to the racecourse, where I was the appointed roving reporter for all four afternoons of the meeting. I don't think I have ever had a more exhilarating or enjoyable working experience. In some ways it was like being with Channel 4 because there was an amazing camaraderie within the team, and as a radio team is so much smaller than a television team, it felt even more intense. To increase that feeling of a happy union – and also to save licence-fee payers' money – most of us stayed together in a farmhouse that the Beeb had rented for the week. Somebody came in to cook us breakfast and dinner, which was always lovely, and we would sit around the table discussing plans for the following day. I had some smashing conversations with our lead presenter, the excellent John Inverdale. We swapped stories about the people we had met and I have to say I learned an awful lot just from sitting next to him at dinner. And isn't it great that even at my age you can still learn new things? I found Invers to be a fascinating person. When you watch him on TV or listen to him on radio he comes across as so laid-back and cool, but in some ways he is the most intense person I've ever met. He also told me that whenever he is travelling to a sporting venue he tries to listen to the same piece of music as he knows it puts him in the right mood.

The really hard part of the job was that while I was roving around the racecourse I had to wear an enormous radio appliance on my back in a rucksack. Dear God it was heavy. By the end of each day I was knackered as I must have covered more miles in a day than a runner in the National Hunt Chase. I was also told at the end of the opening afternoon that Channel 4 had made a complaint because I had been constantly getting into their picture shots when I was interviewing winning jockeys coming back up the famous walkway. I honestly didn't mean for it to happen. I'm not saying I'm not glad it happened but I didn't do it on purpose.

One thing that was different on the BBC was that I was no longer Tommo. Or at least I wasn't supposed to be. The 5 live bosses were keen that I was known as Derek not Tommo, so every time the word Tommo came out I had to pay £5 to the Injured Jockeys Fund. I got through seven Tommos in the first five minutes. There were also quite a few 'big fellas' along the way. I do say 'big fella' quite a lot. It all stems from a day way back when I was working with Brough and was approaching a very popular but extremely tiny horse called Le Garcon d'Or. As I greeted him I said, 'hey big fella', which Brough thought was hilarious as the horse was barely bigger than a pony. There and then the catchphrase stuck and I've been calling people 'big fella' ever since. People seem to enjoy me saying it but I also increasingly say it for a reason. I can't remember anyone's name. I see people I know and in my brain there is just a big empty space. Instead of insulting them I call them 'big fella' and they have always been none the wiser. Until now that is!

One person I called something else was Noel Edmonds, who royally stitched me up and presented me with a 'Gotcha Oscar' on his BBC1 Saturday night programme *Noel's House Party*, which I was also very fond of due to my admiration for Mr Blobby. Even now, when I think of that pink, bouncy bundle of fun saying, 'Blobby, Blobby, Blobby' all the time it makes me giggle. I actually once got to meet the person inside Mr Blobby and it turned out he was nothing like the character he was playing.

The reason I was set up by Noel was partly my fault. The previous year at Kempton I had been talking to him near the Channel 4 presenting position. As I took the show into a commercial break I asked Noel if he could just stand in my place while I went for a quick pee. I told him I would be back in two shakes. I made sure I wasn't and Noel had to take over for the first ten seconds after the adverts. He told me he would get his revenge and he did.

Maybe I'm naive but I suspected nothing. About a year later a woman rang from the BBC and asked me if I would be interested in hosting the pilot for a new Sunday night religion programme. She said it would be based around village life in a different place each week and that it could eventually take over from *Songs of Praise*. The problem for me was that the day of filming coincided with a *Channel 4 Racing* day at Newmarket. I pointed that out to the lady, but, much to my surprise, she said that she had already spoken to Andrew Franklin and he was happy to release me. I was mortified. I didn't want to give up a day of paid work for Channel 4, but when I spoke to Andrew he said this could be very good for my career so he insisted I do the pilot.

I had to drive to a little village just outside Watford, where all the residents seemed to be bordering on barmy. When I got there I was shown a running order that involved me taking part in a medieval re-enactment that the villagers apparently staged once a year. It was all a bit knights of the round table and to join in I had to dress up like Sir Lancelot in a suit of armour. I still hadn't cottoned on to what was going on. They made me sit on a horse and then take part in a 'fight to the death' with another knight. We had a sword-fighting instructor who showed me what to do, but when we started filming the fight the other knight groaned and fell down to the ground.

'Christ, what have you done?' the director said. 'You've killed him, Tommo.'

The medics rushed to the scene and people kept saying not to move him. I was shocked. I was supposed to be filming a successor to *Songs of Praise* but it looked as though I'd committed manslaughter. A few seconds later I felt like committing murder because the helmet of the prostrate knight was removed and I saw Noel Edmonds looking up at me, saying: 'Gotcha!'

And do you know the worst part? It was having to give up that day's work at Newmarket.

TWENTY

WHAT I AM

I have told you what I have done and I have told you what I still do. I have told you the person I used to be and now must tell you the person I am today.

I am Derek but I am also Tommo. I am one but I am also the other. Tommo is what you see. Derek is saved for those closest to me. Please don't think, though, that the man you see on the television or at the racecourse is a fake. He is not. I do not pretend to be anything when I am at work. What you see is me being me. It's simply that a part of me, almost certainly the largest part of me, comes alive when I work. When I go home, or when I'm with family and friends, that part of me rests, but show me a microphone and I can snap back into action in an instant.

I don't often get angry, but if I'm in a bit of a mood at home, or in the middle of an argument with Julie, and the phone rings, I pick it up, say hello and can then be almost immediately the 'ho-ho-ho' Tommo that everyone knows so well. In that way I am two people wrapped up into one but both are real. Julie knows me better than anyone. She knows my faults and would list them to you one by one if you asked her, but nobody gets angrier than my wife if I get called false. She hates it and I hate it as well. When my critics suggest that Tommo is an act they are accusing me of trying to pull the wool over people's eyes, which I would never do. It's a cliche, but I am just a working class lad from Middlesbrough who did okay. I try to be nice to everyone I meet, not just because I would hope they might be nice back to me, but because I think that's how a person ought to be. If people come up to me in the street and start talking to me I would never ignore them. If somebody wants to have a chat with me I feel flattered. It shows that maybe I've been doing my job right.

So Derek is real and so is Tommo. There is, however, a difference between the two. More often than not Tommo will have a microphone in his hand. Derek will not. When I'm holding a microphone I am completely comfortable. If I'm broadcasting I am generally at ease. I will interview anyone or anything. There is very little I will not do in the name of work and I'll nearly always do it with a smile on my face. But it's easy to get the wrong impression of a person. Believe it or not, I'm actually quite shy. When I'm working it's hard to faze me, but if I walk into a room full of people that I don't know and the environment is unfamiliar I hide in my shell. All the confidence drains from me. Yet if someone walked into that room with a microphone, camera and sound equipment and asked me to talk, I would flower in front of your eyes.

That can only mean that I love to perform and I don't deny it. I also cannot deny that I am on the careful side with money. Julie often tells me that I'm not so much careful as mean, but I'd like to think there is more to it than that. Regrettably, the evidence against me is plentiful. I once took Julie to Paris for a weekend break that would end on the Sunday with me working at the Prix de l'Arc de

Triomphe. While we were on the plane I suggested that we spend Saturday lunchtime having a picnic somewhere romantic, which Julie thought was a lovely idea. I had gained valuable brownie points. Julie freshened herself up in the hotel while I went out and got the goodies for the picnic. So far so good, but not long after we got to our chosen picnic point it all went wrong. The problem was I had only bought a baguette. Everything else I had collected from the plane. They had freebies galore on board the flight, and with all those little bags of nuts and biscuits going begging, it seemed silly to spend good money on more food. Julie did not see it quite the same way. It turned into a decidedly frosty couple of days.

Linked to my attitude to money is my attitude to work. I work so hard because I worry the phone might one day stop ringing. I worry that if I say no to a job, the person who has asked me will not ask me again. I work through a love of work but also through a fear that one day I might not be wanted. I feel like an athlete who is in a never-ending pursuit of a gold medal that forever remains just out of reach. Julie would be the first to admit that she would not want me at home all the time. She says that if I was she might hang herself. The problem is that I have never managed to strike the right balance between a working life and a home life. I know that better than anyone. I agree with Julie that because I work so hard we don't really have a family life, yet everything I do is done for the sake of the family. It's true that I get an enormous kick out of working, but first and foremost I put work above family for the sake of the family.

I realise I should spend more quality time at home. I accept that instead of commentating at Yarmouth I would be better off spending ten minutes kicking a ball with my son. Regrettably, I cannot convince myself that reducing my workload would be the right thing to do. I know that if William Hill or Betfred rang me up and offered a job I could turn it down without any consequences because I do enough work for them for that to be possible. But I don't turn them down. The problem in my eyes is that all I have is me. I cannot sell steel like dad did and my brother Howard continues to do. I have nothing to sell but myself. All I have to offer the world is Tommo and therefore Tommo has to be constantly available. I am the brand. I have to exploit Tommo as well as I possibly can.

When dad died I felt alone for the first time in my life. I wasn't alone, because when he passed away I was still surrounded by family, friends and loved ones, but I did feel alone and I did feel scared. It was as though a safety net that had always been there had suddenly been removed. Since then I have felt compelled to work. I want to make certain that when I die Julie and the children will want for nothing. Julie and I both thought that having cancer would change me for the better but in some ways it has changed me for the worse. Whereas for some people, surviving cancer would make them want to enjoy life more than ever before, for me it has just increased my desire to work. Cancer made me confront my mortality face to face. I was closer than I ever have been to dying and that has made me more determined than ever to make sure I safeguard my family's future wellbeing while I'm still able to do so.

Although I accept I should spend more time with my family, that does not for a second mean that I do not cherish my family. I would have loved dad to have been alive for more of my television career, and I continue to miss him, but it's great that I can still go back north to see mum and Howard. They mean the world to me. Moreover, I am immensely proud of my family. Alex and James, my sons with Janie, both had difficult childhoods, and to a significant degree I was responsible for making them difficult. It is to my great delight that I have wonderful relationships with both the boys. They have turned into fine young men. As individuals they are very different but that doesn't stop them from being extremely close to each other.

Alex has proved a real success in the business world and has shown himself to be forward-thinking and astute. He is also a bit tight, which probably helps in his line of work. He sometimes comes with me on racing trips and if it's a choice between eating in a top-notch restaurant or a burger joint he'll opt for the burger joint every time. He's my kind of boy. Intriguingly, Alex speaks with an English accent. So do I. His brother James, or Jim as plenty of people call him, does not and instead has a Scottish accent. He also has my looks, for which I know he's grateful. In fact he has bared almost everything except his soul for a charity calendar with his team-mates. When I worked for *Channel 4 Racing* we also did a calendar but nobody ever asked me to pose topless. James might sound different to his old man but you can see Tommo in his face. Whenever I see him play rugby I feel pride filling my body and fortunately for me he is now playing on my side of the border for London Scottish. He really is very good indeed. He recently competed in the World Cup Sevens event for the third time and last year, with his dad watching in the stands of Dublin's Aviva Stadium, he scored a try for his then club, Edinburgh, in the Heineken Cup semi-final. I was elated. I turned to the man sat next to me and said: 'That's my son.'

India is my favourite daughter. I always tell her that and it always gets her annoyed. Like her mother, she is an absolute stunner. She has some of me in her somewhere, I've just never been able to see where. Like her brother, Hugo, she has been very lucky and has attended an excellent private school, but she works hard and is also pretty grounded. Whenever she goes to a car boot sale she makes more money than anyone else, so she knows the value of a pound coin, which pleases me. Jamie Spencer has told me more than once that his son, Charlie, wants to marry her. That's lovely, but unfortunately Charlie is only six.

Hugo is a smashing young lad and for someone aged only ten is astonishingly bright. He never stops asking questions, which I love, because people who are like that want to learn. I meet a lot of youngsters while I'm doing my job, and I'm always happy to let someone who wants some work experience follow me for a day. I reckon I'm pretty good at spotting the ones who will make it and the ones who will not, and I'm very confident Hugo will make it. He is already practically fluent in Latin, which I find remarkable. He says he wants to be a barrister but he could easily end up as the chief executive of a PLC or a future prime minister. He is also very much a boy turning into a man. We were in a newsagent's shop the other day and he picked up a copy of *The Sun*, opened it at page three, showed it me and asked me what I thought of the young lady on show. I don't know where he gets that from, I really don't.

Julie probably hopes Hugo does not turn out quite like his dad, but for all my failings, and despite not spending enough time with the children, she says that I am nonetheless a fantastic father. In return, I say with absolute sincerity that she is a both a magnificent mother and a wonderful wife. This will come as a shock, but Derek Thompson is not always the easiest person to have as your husband. Julie puts up with me with tremendous courage, endless patience and considerable understanding. She is my harshest critic but more importantly also my most loyal supporter. I owe her so much. Julie will be delighted to read that I am extremely confident my third wife will turn out to be my last wife. Unless, that is, she gets an offer from Sir Tom Jones, who she is madly in love with and who she insisted we see in concert on consecutive nights on our Las Vegas honeymoon. She also got to meet him backstage and had her picture taken with his arm around her. I couldn't compete.

There have been times when I have not been the husband to Julie I should have been. When Julie's mother died she was devastated. It was the hardest thing she had ever been through. My reaction to her grief was to carry on as normal. I found it impossible to provide the emotional support she needed. My way of dealing with a major problem, including being told I had cancer, is to put the unwanted and difficult thoughts to the back of my mind. I try as hard as I can to pretend they are not there and then continue as if nothing had happened. It works for me but it does not work for everyone. I find confronting my own emotions hard enough. Dealing head on with the emotions of others is even harder.

Julie says even a top psychiatrist or psychologist would struggle to get to the bottom of me and she is probably right. She says I lack any emotional depths and she is probably right about that as well. After dad died I knew I had to be strong and perhaps it's true that since then I have felt I cannot afford to let down my guard. It could also be true that I believe showing emotion represents weakness. What is not true, though, is that I am incapable of feeling emotion. When Alex and James were growing up and were heading home after spending a precious weekend with me I would cry as soon as I had waved them goodbye at the airport.

I would then cry all the way back to the car. Never once, though, would I have allowed myself to cry in front of the boys. I can get upset and I do get upset, and sometimes it is over little things that people say about me, good and bad. It has been said that I have the hide of a rhinoceros, but although I revel in knockabout humour and love nothing more than people pulling my leg, I get hurt when I am attacked for no good reason. Sometimes the odd jibe does get through to me. I might not always open my shirt to show the wounds but that does not mean they are not there. I am more sensitive than people realise.

Most of the snide comments that have come my way have been directed at me from people in racing. I am well aware that I am not everyone's cup of tea. I know that for some I am a bit over the top and a little too populist, but I also like to think that there are plenty of people out there who like what I do and the way I do it. Josh Apiafi, a great mate who has made a massive success out of Jockey Club Racecourses' Rewards For Racing initiative, once wrote a letter to the *Racing Post*, in which he said: 'Tommo gets knocked sometimes but he is the best person in the world to bring racing to the man in the street.' And that's what I try to do. I wish that even those who do not like me or my style of presenting would accept that I have racing's best interests at heart. I want people to love racing, and whether I have been speaking to them on Channel 4, At The Races, Tommo TV or BBC Radio, I have always sought to put across my own genuine love of the sport. I have worked hard in racing, I have earned a very good living out of racing and, more often than not, I have liked the people I have met in racing. But I have not liked everyone, and it is with regret that I have to say some of those I have the least time for live within a few miles of my own front door.

Most racing folk understand that it is through people like myself and other broadcasters and journalists that we connect them to the racing fans and punters who effectively pay their wages. Those who do not understand this are, I believe, failing the sport. Some of those people are among the Newmarket training fraternity and there is no doubt in my mind that those very same trainers, as well as some other individuals at the heart of racing, see themselves as better than someone like me. I know full well that they look down on me in a snobbish way and I find that sad. Sometimes the attitudes of others have made me feel like an outsider in the town where I live, but it doesn't really bother me because I have plenty of friends both out of racing as well as in it.

There are some great racing people in Newmarket that I like very much, people like Frankie Dettori, Saeed Bin Suroor, Simon Crisford, Richard Hills, Michael Hills and my new neighbour Paul Hanagan. Outside of Newmarket there are few people I respect more than Mark Johnston. I doubt anybody in racing is as busy as Mark, and his work ethic is quite extraordinary, but I don't think he has ever declined when I have requested an interview. The same is true of his wife Deirdre, his son Charlie and his staff. Mark has revolutionised the art of training and the way a training business can operate, but he has never let success go to his head. I like and admire him very much indeed. The same is true of the leading jump racing personalities like Tony McCoy, Paul Nicholls and Nicky Henderson.

As I write the final words of this book, I also want to repeat how much I owe to Andrew Franklin, my *Channel 4 Racing* boss for so many years. He was a constant ally. I shall always be grateful to him, as I shall to my best mate Bob Champion. Through thick and thin, good times and bad, he has been my rock and not once has he let me down. For almost all my life he has been there for me and I have been a better, happier and wiser person because of that.

And so who is that person? He is Derek and he is Tommo. He is the man who used to go on the knacker man's wagon to Redcar racecourse and ended up presenting racing for *World of Sport* from the very same track. I am the man who in 1973 became the youngest ever commentator in Grand National history and then 40 years later returned to my BBC Radio roots for a memorable Cheltenham Festival. I am the man who presented racing on terrestrial television for more than three decades, the man who was *The Morning Line*'s host for most of its life, the man who did a bit of everything for *Channel 4 Racing*, saved *Channel 4 Racing* and was then sacked by *Channel 4 Racing*. I am the man who opened a betting shop near you, the man with the lucky bucket in his hand and the smile on his face. I am the man who got embroiled in the kidnapping of Shergar, the man who tried to make sense of synchronised swimming at the Olympics and the man who got the weather a bit wrong when confusing a Dubai World Cup night monsoon for a passing shower. I have been sworn at by Rod Stewart, had a door slammed in my face by Bo Derek and enjoyed conversations with JR Ewing, Eric Morecambe and the Queen. I am also the man who prevented her son, the future king, from winning a race at Plumpton. Fortunately, neither she nor he held a grudge.

I survived cancer, I am still alive and I intend to carry on both living and working for as long as I possibly can. For this very lucky big fella, it has not been a bad life. It has been outstanding.

ACKNOWLEDGEMENTS

As Derek's writing partner in this book I wish to place on record my thanks to some of those who helped the project reach the printed page.

Derek's wife Julie could not have done more to assist her husband and his ghostwriter in their endeavours and deserves a special mention, as does Derek's mother, Lilian, and brother Howard.

Bob Champion was an invaluable source of material, as were Derek's broadcasting colleagues Andrew Franklin, Brough Scott and John Francome. Thanks are also due to the BBC's Frank Keogh for supplying some of his own Tommo-related material, while Derek would be most upset if I did not pass on gratitude to Glenn Tubby for the book's title.

Finally, sincere thanks to the excellent Racing Post Books team. Without the work, time, dedication and expertise of James de Wesselow, Julian Brown, Liz Ampairee, Sean Magee and John Schwartz at Soapbox this book would not have been produced. Similar thanks go to the Racing Post's Jay Vincent and John Hopkins for their hard work.

INDEX

265